LAND

PEOPLE

NATION

SINCE 1865

A HISTORY OF THE UNITED STATES

LAND

PEOPLE

NATION

SINCE 1865

SECOND EDITION

Anna Uhl Chamot

Kathleen Anderson Steeves

Longman

Land, People, Nation: A History of the United States Since 1865

Pearson Education, 10 Bank Street, White Plains, NY 10606

Editorial director: Ed Lamprich
Senior development editor: Virginia Bernard
Development editor: Elise Pritchard
Senior production editor: Kathleen Silloway
Art director: Patricia Wosczyk
Marketing manager: Alexandra Smith
Production manager: Ray Keating
Senior manufacturing buyer: Edith Pullman
Cover design: Patricia Wosczyk
Cover photos: Bob Pool, Tom Stack and Associates, Inc. (top); Ken Kavanagh, Photo
  Researchers, Inc. (bottom L); Ulrike Welsch, Photo Researchers, Inc. (bottom R)
Text design: Patricia Wosczyk
Icons: Jill Lehan
Text composition: Wendy Wolf
Text font: Minion 12.5/15, Times 12.5/14, Stone Sans 10.5/12.5
Maps: Map Resources, adaptations by Wendy Wolf
Illustrations: Dan Rosandich
Text credits: see pages 160–161

Library of Congress Cataloging-in-Publication Data

Chamot, Anna Uhl.
    Land, People, Nation: A History of the United States / Anna Uhl Chamot, Kathleen
Anderson Steeves.
    p. cm.
    Includes index.
    Summary: An overview of United States history written for speakers of English as a
second language.
    ISBN 0-13-042560-5 (v. 1: pbk.)—ISBN 0-13-042572-9 (v. 2: pbk.)
    1. Readers—United States. 2. United States—History—Problems, exercises, etc. 3.
English language—Textbooks for foreign speakers.
    [1. Readers. 2. United States—History. 3. English language—Textbooks for foreign
speakers.] I. Steeves, Kathleen Anderson. II. Title.
    PE1127.H5C48 2004
    428.6'4—dc22

                                                                            2003022621

ISBN: 0-13-042572-9

LONGMAN ON THE **WEB**

Longman.com offers online resources for
teachers and students. Access our Companion
Websites, our online catalog, and our local
offices around the world.

Visit us at **longman.com**.

Printed in the United States of America
3 4 5 6 7 8 9 10–VHG–08 07 06 05

Contents

List of Maps

To the Teacher

Land, People, Nation: A History of the United States is designed specifically to help prepare English language learners for curricular work in U.S. history and geography. It is also helpful for any students who need to develop learning strategies for these content areas.

The Cognitive Academic Language Learning Approach (CALLA) provides the theoretical and organizational framework for this program. The CALLA model is based on social-cognitive theory and integrates standards-based content, academic language development, and explicit instruction in learning strategies. The CALLA instructional sequence consists of five recursive phases: Preparation, Presentation, Practice, Self-Evaluation, and Expansion.

- **Preparation**—Students engage in activities designed to activate their prior knowledge, develop essential content vocabulary, and pique their curiosity about the topic to be studied.

- **Presentation**—The teacher and the text provide new information about the history or geography of the United States.

- **Practice**—Students engage in activities that further their understanding of the concepts presented, often through collaborative work with classmates.

- **Self-Evaluation**—Students think about what they have learned and assess how well they have internalized the concepts presented.

- **Expansion**—Students think in depth about historical events and apply the lessons of history to their own lives.

Content

The first book in the program, *Land, People, Nation: A History of the United States, Beginnings to 1877,* provides an overview of the early years of exploration and settlement in the part of North America that was to become the United States; the establishment of a new nation; westward expansion; and the Civil War and Reconstruction. Interwoven with this historical survey is the study of geographic regions of the United States and its territories.

The second book in the program, *Land, People, Nation: A History of the United States Since 1865,* surveys the period of industrialization in the late nineteenth and early twentieth centuries; the development of the nation as a global power; wars and conflict; the prosperity and economic hardships of the mid- to late-twentieth century; and the search for democracy and equality for its people up to the present.

Academic Language

The academic language component of *Land, People, Nation: A History of the United States* focuses on the language skills that students need in history and geography. These include reading and listening for information, analyzing photographs and maps for information, demonstrating comprehension, researching and writing reports on historical figures, and giving oral presentations.

The language activities preceding and following the readings develop academic language skills while reinforcing understanding of the content. Students gain a basic history and geography vocabulary (see the Glossary at the end of each book), and develop and practice a variety of learning strategies and reading skills. Listening comprehension in the academic context is also emphasized. In each unit, students listen to a "mini-lecture" and are guided through note-taking skills. The texts for these mini-lectures are provided in the *Teacher's Guide*.

Many of the activities in these books involve students working in pairs or small groups, and provide them the opportunities to use language actively. Discussion questions, in addition to a variety of other activities requiring social interaction, provide creative springboards for the development of thinking skills and oral language.

Learning Strategies

Learning strategies are specific techniques that students can use independently to understand, remember, and apply both informational content and language skills. Although some students acquire effective learning strategies on their own, many students (both native and non-native English speakers) can benefit from explicit instruction in these techniques. Explicit instruction includes naming the strategy, explaining why it is useful and how to use it, and asking students to practice it with a particular learning task, such as reading, writing, or listening.

Learning strategies and U.S. history and geography standards addressed in each unit of *Land, People, Nation: A History of the United States* are provided at the end of each book. The first mention of a particular strategy introduces and describes the strategy and indicates how it can help the student with the current task. The strategy is then recycled at regular intervals and students are asked to identify the strategy described for a task. Later, suggestions are provided for students to combine strategies and/or choose the strategy or strategies they will use for a particular task. This sequence is repeated in each book. The learning strategy sequence is designed to prompt both students and teachers to talk about strategies and explore ways in which they can be applied.

Teacher's Guide

Land, People, Nation: A History of the United States can be used effectively in both intermediate ESOL classrooms and in the U.S. history class in middle school and high school. The *Teacher's Guide* presents detailed lesson plans for each student book. By following these lesson plans, you will provide your students not only with a solid conceptual base in U.S. history that is aligned to the National History Standards but also with many opportunities to use their developing English skills. In addition, you will be helping them to build a valuable inventory of learning strategies that will be useful not only in history and geography but also in other content areas requiring skilled reading, writing, and listening comprehension.

The *Teacher's Guide* also includes suggested answers for all student exercises and activities as well as historical thinking and application activities for each unit.

Land, People, Nation: A History of the United States assists students in learning the important concepts, academic language, and learning strategies essential to the study of history.

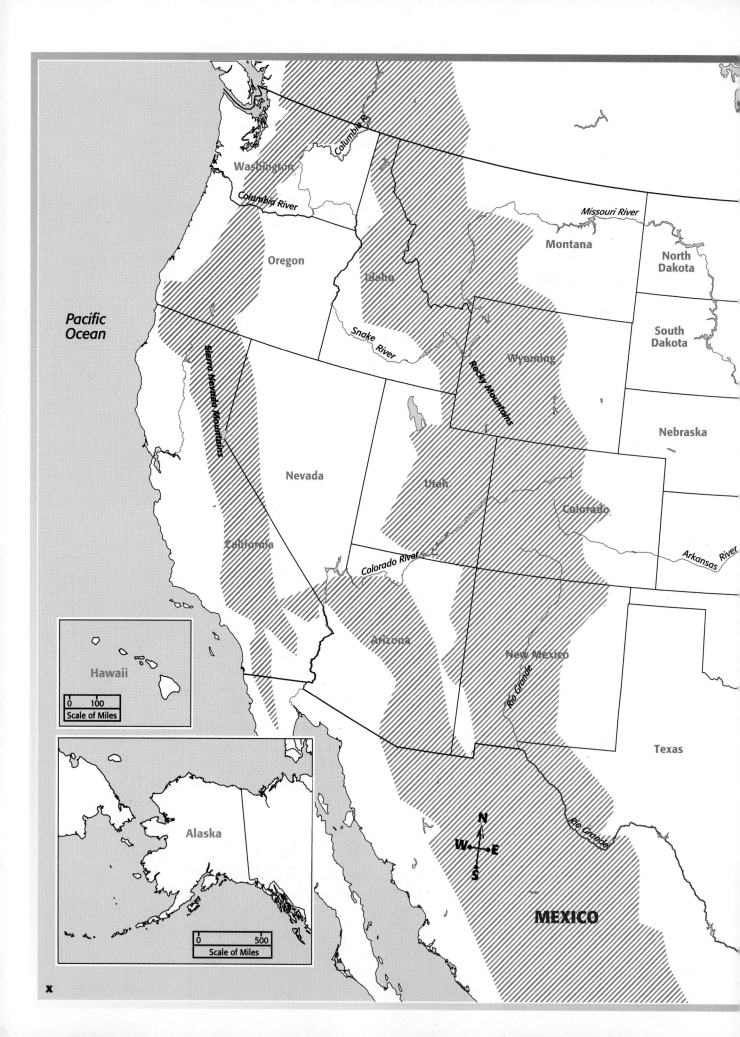

Pacific
Ocean

Washington

Columbia R.

Columbia River

Oregon

Idaho

Snake River

Sierra Nevada Mountains

Nevada

California

Colorado River

Arizona

Montana

Missouri River

North Dakota

South Dakota

Wyoming

Rocky Mountains

Utah

Colorado

Arkansas River

Nebraska

New Mexico

Rio Grande

Texas

Rio Grande

MEXICO

N
W   E
S

Hawaii

0   100
Scale of Miles

Alaska

0   500
Scale of Miles

LAND

PEOPLE

NATION

SINCE 1865

Industrialization and Change: 1865–1900

Tell what you think

Beginning in the early part of the nineteenth century, more and more things were made by machines in factories, instead of by hand in people's homes. This change is called the *Industrial Revolution*.

- What changes in people's lives do you think were caused by the Industrial Revolution?

- What do you think happened to Native Americans and former slaves after the Civil War?

- Who do you think were the new immigrants to the United States after 1865?

Write your ideas in your notebook.

In this unit you will

- read about the ways in which the United States grew after the Civil War

- learn about some important U.S. industries and inventions

- learn about the Grassland and Desert regions

- find out about some important people in the West

- learn about the lives of rich and poor people

- study some people who tried to help workers and poor people

- use maps, charts, and graphs

- sharpen your listening, speaking, and note-taking skills

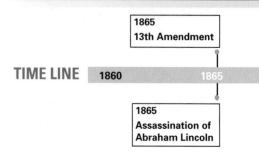

TIME LINE | 1860 | 1865

1865
13th Amendment

1865
Assassination of
Abraham Lincoln

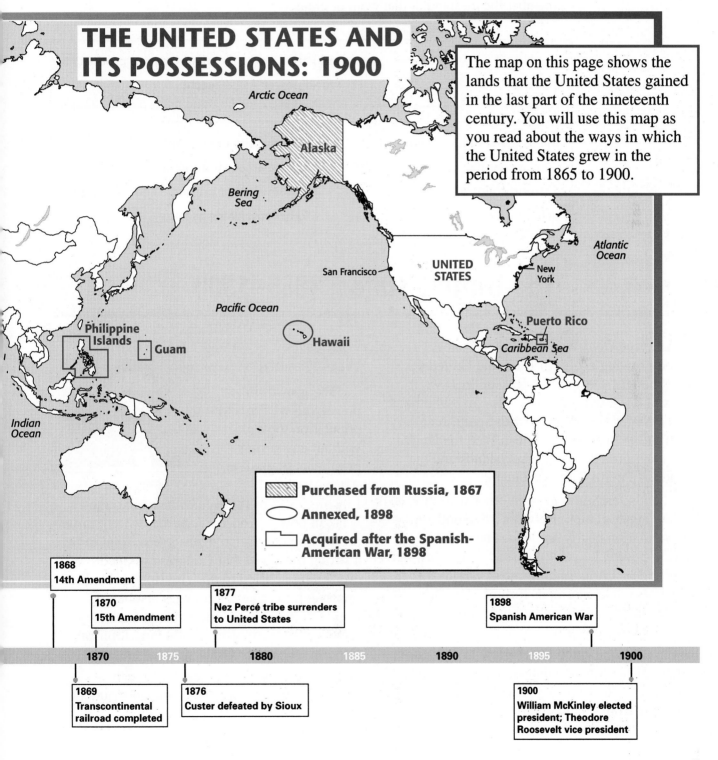

THE UNITED STATES AND ITS POSSESSIONS: 1900

Arctic Ocean

Alaska

Bering Sea

The map on this page shows the lands that the United States gained in the last part of the nineteenth century. You will use this map as you read about the ways in which the United States grew in the period from 1865 to 1900.

Atlantic Ocean

UNITED STATES

San Francisco

New York

Pacific Ocean

Philippine Islands

Guam

Hawaii

Puerto Rico

Caribbean Sea

Indian Ocean

▨ **Purchased from Russia, 1867**

◯ **Annexed, 1898**

▢ **Acquired after the Spanish-American War, 1898**

1868
14th Amendment

1870
15th Amendment

1877
Nez Percé tribe surrenders to United States

1898
Spanish American War

| 1870 | 1875 | 1880 | 1885 | 1890 | 1895 | 1900 |

1869
Transcontinental railroad completed

1876
Custer defeated by Sioux

1900
William McKinley elected president; Theodore Roosevelt vice president

LEARNING STRATEGY

When you draw, look at, or imagine a picture to help you remember the meaning of a word, you are using the learning strategy **using imagery**.

Work with a classmate. Discuss the meanings of the vocabulary words in the top box. In your notebook, write the correct definition from the lower box next to each word or phrase. Finally, draw a small picture or symbol next to each word that will help you remember the meaning of that word or phrase.

double	fortune	industry	manufactured products
poverty	wealthy	world power	yacht

things made in factories	the opposite of wealth
large, expensive boat	a large amount of money
a strong country	a business that produces and sells things
rich	to become twice as large

The United States, 1865–1900

After the Civil War, the United States started growing again. In 1867, the United States bought Alaska from Russia. In 1898, it annexed (took over) Hawaii. Also in 1898, the United States fought a war with Spain. As a result of the Spanish-American War, the United States acquired the Philippine Islands and the islands of Puerto Rico and Guam.

The United States grew in other ways, too. It grew in population: Between 1870 and 1900, the population nearly doubled. The country grew in power: Its navy was the third largest in the world in 1900. And it grew in wealth: Its industries made enormous fortunes for some people, and its manufactured products were used all over the world.

Finally, the United States grew in literature and art. U.S. writers, painters, and architects were admired not only by Americans but also by people from other countries.

POLITICS: WEAK PRESIDENTS

Andrew Johnson

The growth in power and wealth and population took place without any strong presidents to guide it. After Abraham Lincoln, most of the presidents were quite weak in power. Andrew Johnson, who became president when Lincoln was killed, tried to be a strong president, but Congress stopped everything he tried to do. The House voted to impeach him (charge him with disobeying laws) but the Senate failed by one vote to remove him from office. Following Johnson, General Ulysses S. Grant became president.

During these years there was much corruption in government. Some government workers stole money from the government. Grant himself was an honest man, but many of the friends he gave jobs to were dishonest.

There was also corruption in city and state governments. In New York City, Mayor Tweed (who was known as "Boss Tweed") was very powerful. He had control of all the business in the city. He often got people to vote for him because he could find jobs for them.

"Boss Tweed"

ECONOMICS: THE RICH AND THE POOR

Some people made enormous fortunes between 1865 and 1900. John D. Rockefeller made a billion dollars in the oil industry. Andrew Carnegie made hundreds of millions of dollars in the steel industry. William H. Vanderbilt made more millions in railroads. J. Pierpont Morgan built up a huge banking company. These were only a few of the people who became extremely wealthy during this period.

Most Americans did not get rich, however. Millions of men and women worked in noisy, dirty factories for twelve to fourteen hours a day for very little money. Many of these workers were immigrants who came from other countries. Some people weren't able to find work and had no money at all. Many Americans lived in tenements—crowded, cold apartments without running water or heat.

SOCIETY: THE GILDED AGE

A popular book written in the 1870s by Mark Twain and Charles Warner was called *The Gilded Age*. To gild something is to put a thin layer of gold on it. Underneath the gold, however, there is just ordinary wood, plaster, or metal. The period from 1865 to 1900 was like this. What many people saw were the great houses of the wealthy, their powerful steam yachts, and the huge parties that they gave for one another. But underneath all this were greed, corruption, and poverty. There was a huge gap between the rich and the poor. This was the Gilded Age.

UNDERSTANDING WHAT YOU READ **Summarizing**

A good way to remember information is to write down the important ideas in your own words. This learning strategy is called **summarizing**.

LEARNING STRATEGY

Use the questions below to write a summary of the reading. Remember to use your own words. Write your summary in your notebook.

1. In what four ways did the United States change from 1865 to 1900?

2. What three problems did the United States have during this time?

3. Who were four men who became very wealthy during this period, and how did they make their money?

4. Why was this period of U.S. history called "The Gilded Age"?

UNDERSTANDING WHAT YOU READ **Using Maps**

Turn to the map on page 3. In your notebook, make a list of the new territories the United States acquired between 1867 and 1900. Write down the date it acquired each one, and how it acquired each one.

What Was the Industrial Revolution?

A revolution is a complete change in something. The War for Independence, which started in 1775, is called the American Revolution because it was a complete change in government. After the American Revolution in the United States, another type of revolution happened. This was the Industrial Revolution.

The Industrial Revolution was a complete change in the way that things were made. Before the Industrial Revolution, most things were made by hand in people's homes or in small shops. After the Industrial Revolution, the use of natural resources (iron, coal, oil, wood) increased. Most things were made by machines in factories. The machines could make things faster and more cheaply.

You are going to read about four important industries that developed during the Industrial Revolution and about some of the changes these industries made in the United States. The four industries are *textiles*, or the making of cloth, *railroads*, *steel*, and *oil*.

THE TEXTILE INDUSTRY

The first industry that used machines in the United States was the textile industry. The first textile factory opened in 1790. Fifty years later, in 1840, there were 1,200 textile factories in the United States. Most of these were in the Northeast.

Irish and Chinese workers build the last mile of the transcontinental railroad.

Women working in a textile factory

Towns and cities grew up around the factories. The factories made cloth from the cotton grown in the South. The textile factory workers were mostly women. These women left the farms where they grew up and moved to the cities.

THE RAILROADS

The first railroad companies started in 1830 in South Carolina and Maryland. By 1836, there were railroads in eleven states, with more than a thousand miles of track.

In 1869, a railroad across the whole country was completed. It connected the East Coast to the West Coast, and it was called the transcontinental railroad. Many of the people who built this railroad were immigrants from China, Japan, and Ireland. Railroads to the West made it easier for people from the East to settle in the West. The railroads also carried products made by the factories, and crops grown on the farms and plantations.

THE STEEL INDUSTRY

Steel is made out of iron, but it is stronger than ordinary iron. People used steel long before the Industrial Revolution, but it was very expensive to make. Then, in the mid-1800s, an Englishman named Bessemer invented a cheap way to make iron into steel. At the same time, Americans discovered large amounts of iron near Lake Superior. This iron was made into steel in huge factories, and the steel was used to build bridges, railroads, and many other things. By 1900, the United States produced more steel than any other country.

THE OIL INDUSTRY

Oil was first found in the United States in 1859, in Pennsylvania. The Pennsylvania oil was first used to make the machines in factories run smoothly. Oils made from animals and plants had been used before this, but the oil from the ground was cheaper and worked better. This oil also burned well, so people used it for lighting lamps. People learned how to make oil into gasoline. They used the gasoline to run the new machines and, later, automobiles. By 1900, oil was a big industry in the United States.

One of the first oil wells in Pennsylvania

UNDERSTANDING BAR GRAPHS

LEARNING STRATEGY

When you study (or make) a graph or chart, you are using the learning strategy **graphic organizer**. This strategy helps you understand facts and relationships between facts.

Study the bar graph and then answer the questions in your notebook. Remember that the numbers at the bottom of the graph represent thousands of miles. This means that you should read *200* as "two hundred thousand miles."

Using the Bessemer process in a steel factory

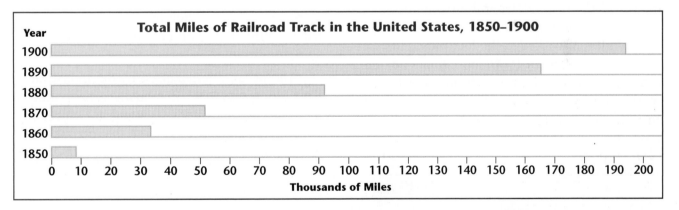

Total Miles of Railroad Track in the United States, 1850–1900

1. About how many thousands of miles of railroad track were built by 1850? By 1900?

2. About how many miles of *new* track were built between 1860 and 1870?

3. In which ten years were the most miles of *new* track built? About how many miles of *new* track were built?

4. How many miles of track were needed to cross the United States from San Francisco, California, to New York City? Use an atlas to find this information.

BEFORE YOU READ | Making Predictions

Before you read, think about what you already know and what new information you think will come next. This learning strategy is called **predicting**. It gets you ready to learn new things.

You have read about some of the new industries of the Industrial Revolution. How do you think these inventions and industries changed the lives of American people? Look at these pictures and talk with a classmate or with a small group. Use the pictures to help you think about how life changed with the Industrial Revolution. Write your ideas in your notebook.

Now read the text below to learn about other changes the Industrial Revolution made in American life. See how many of the changes you predicted are mentioned in the text.

Girl working in a Southern cotton mill

THE INDUSTRIAL REVOLUTION BRINGS CHANGE

Before the Industrial Revolution, most people lived on farms or in small towns. After the Industrial Revolution, more people moved to the cities where the factories were.

Work in the factories was hard. Many people worked for twelve to fourteen hours every day, and they did not earn much money. Even children worked in the factories. This was called *child labor*. In 1900, more than one out of every six children in the nation was a factory worker. Factory workers often got sick and died from the long, hard, unsafe work.

A street on the Lower East Side in New York City, 1890s

Because the working conditions were so bad, some people got together to protect themselves. They formed groups called *labor unions* to try to get better conditions and more pay. They asked for laws to protect the children who worked in the factories. If they did not get what they asked for, the union members stopped working. When the factory owners tried to hire other workers, there was sometimes violence.

Another problem caused by the Industrial Revolution was that some businesses became so large that small businesses could not succeed. When one business is so large that no one else can compete with it, it is called a *monopoly*. In the early 1900s, the government made laws to prohibit monopolies, but these laws did not always work.

The Industrial Revolution changed life in some good ways. Many things became cheaper, and more people could buy them. The United States also sold more products to other countries.

As the Industrial Revolution continued, inventors thought of more ways to do things differently. Some inventions made work faster, some made work easier. This also made the products less expensive to buy. By 1900, people were using new inventions like electric lights, telephones, typewriters, and phonographs. Some people were even driving automobiles. Life in America had certainly changed! In the years to come, it would change even more.

Early phonograph

UNDERSTANDING WHAT YOU READ | Completing a Study Chart

LEARNING STRATEGY

Reminder: Completing a study chart will help you recall important facts. A study chart is one type of **graphic organizer**.

Look at the study chart below. Copy the chart in your notebook. Important dates in the Industrial Revolution are written in the left column. In the center column, write what happened on each date and where it happened. In the right column, write why it was important. Write the important facts only. You do not have to write complete sentences. Remember, you will find the facts on pages 6 and 7.

Date	What Happened and Where	Why Important
1790		
1830		
mid-1800s		
1859		
1869		

UNDERSTANDING WHAT YOU READ | Cause and Effect

The Industrial Revolution caused many changes in life in the United States. These changes are the *effects* of the Industrial Revolution.

Answer the questions in your notebook.

1. What were some of the good effects of the Industrial Revolution?

2. What were some of the bad effects of the Industrial Revolution?

The Grassland Regions

After the Civil War, in the second half of the 1800s, many people moved west into the central part of the United States. After settlers crossed the Mississippi River, they entered a Grassland Region. First, they traveled on flat ground with high grass. This type of grassland is called a *prairie*. The prairie gets a lot of rain, from twenty to thirty-five inches a year. People who settled on the prairie brought new metal plows and, because of this, they could plant crops of corn and wheat. This area became the best farmland in the United States.

Farther west is an area that today we call the Great Plains. The Great Plains cover the western parts of North Dakota, South Dakota, Nebraska, and Kansas, as well as the eastern part of Montana, Wyoming, and Colorado. This land is higher than the prairie. In the western part of the Great Plains, the grass does not grow very high and there are no trees. This type of grassland is called a *steppe*. There is less rain on the steppe, only ten to twenty inches a year. The steppe is a good region for raising animals that eat grass. Settlers on the Great Plains steppe built ranches and raised cattle and sheep. Farmers grew crops that needed less rain, such as wheat.

There are Grassland Regions in many parts of the world. There are prairies and steppes (also known as plateaus) in many countries. A third type of grassland is called a *savanna*. A savanna is a tropical grassland, near the equator. The soil is not good in the savanna grasslands, so people do not farm. Instead they raise cattle, sheep, and goats—animals that eat the savanna grass.

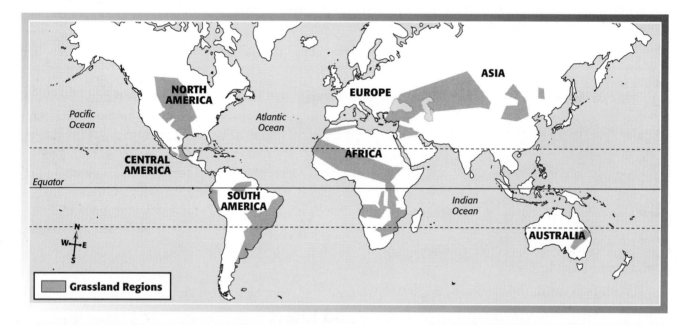

Grassland Regions

UNDERSTANDING WHAT YOU READ **Using Maps**

Look at the map. Answer the questions in your notebook.

1. Which continents have Grassland Regions?

2. Which continents have savannas?

3. List the states that contain Grassland Regions. Use the map on pages x–xi if necessary.

Harvesting wheat

Identifying What You Already Know

**LEARNING
STRATEGY**

You can understand new information better when you think, talk, and write about what you already know about it before you read. This learning strategy is called **use what you know**.

What do you already know about cowboys? Where did they live? What did they do? Talk with a group of classmates about the facts you already know about cowboys. Then talk about new information you would like to learn.

In your notebook, make a *K-W-L-H* chart. Write sentences to complete the *K* (What We Already *K*now) column. Write questions to complete the *W* (What We *W*ant to Find Out) column. You will complete the *L* and *H* columns later.

K	W	L	H

Nat Love, also known as "Deadwood Dick," one of many African Americans who went west after the Civil War to become cowboys

The Cowboy

CATTLE RANCHING ON THE GREAT PLAINS

The steppe lands of the Great Plains were excellent for raising cattle. Some of the people who went west started ranches, or large farms, where they raised cattle and sold them to people in the East who wanted more beef.

THE LONG DRIVE

When the cattle were ready to be sold, the ranchers sent them east by railroad. They hired cowboys to take the cattle from the ranch to the nearest "cow town," where the cattle were put into special railroad cars for the journey east. Some cow towns, such as Abilene and Wichita, Kansas, still exist today.

The journey from the ranch to the cow town was called the "long drive." It was often many hundreds of miles to the railroad, and the long drive could take several months. Stampedes and storms could make it difficult and dangerous.

THE LIFE OF A COWBOY

People today think that cowboys' lives were glamorous and exciting. In fact, the cowboy's life was a hard one. He worked on horseback from sunrise until long after sunset every day, keeping the cattle together and moving.

Cowboys were excellent riders. The youngest cowboy usually took care of the extra horses because cowboys changed horses at least once a day.

The cattle spent the winter out on the grasslands where there were no fences. Each spring, the cowboys rode out on their horses to find and "round up" the cattle. They brought them back into a *corral*, an area with a fence around it. Young cattle had to be branded—that is, a special mark, or *brand*, was burned into their skin. Each ranch had its own brand. If cattle wandered away, the brand showed which ranch the cattle belonged to.

CATTLE RANCHING CHANGES

From 1879 to 1885, there were about 40,000 cowboys working in the West. After 1885, a big change came to ranching. Using a new product called *barbed wire*, farmers built fences to keep cattle off their land. The cattle were no longer able to wander free over the grasslands. Some ranchers started raising sheep instead of cattle. The railroads built more tracks to more places, so cattle could be put onto trains nearer the ranches. The long drives were not necessary anymore.

Using Context

LEARNING STRATEGY

You can make good guesses about what a word means by looking at the context, or the words and sentences that come before and after the new word. This learning strategy is called **making inferences**.

Find the following vocabulary words in "The Cowboy." Look at the words and sentences that come before and after the words. Decide what the words probably mean. Write your definitions in your notebook.

beef	glamorous	sunrise
corral	herd	wander

The inventor Joseph Glidden said of his wire: "Light as air, stronger than whiskey, and cheaper than dirt."

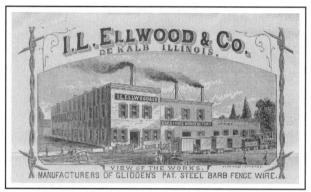

An advertisement for barbed wire

Focusing on What and How You Learned

1. Meet with the same group you worked with to begin your *K-W-L-H* chart in the Before You Read activity on page 11. What new information have you learned about cowboys? Name three jobs that cowboys did. Name three reasons why cowboy life changed after 1885.

2. Read what you wrote in the *K* (What We Already *K*now) column for the activity. Do you need to correct any facts that you listed? Do so now!

3. Read what you wrote in the *W* (What We *W*ant to Find Out) column. Were your questions answered? Check off the questions that were answered. Now look for answers to the questions that still need to be answered. Use an encyclopedia or the Internet.

4. Write sentences in the third column headed *L* (What We *L*earned) to tell what you learned about cowboys.

5. Talk with your classmates about how you learned the new information. Write the learning strategies that all of you used in the fourth column headed *H* (*H*ow We Learned).

6. Share your group's *K-W-L-H* chart with the rest of the class.

Cowboy riding a bucking horse

Work with a partner. Discuss what you already know about Native Americans. Where did they come from? What happened to them when Europeans first arrived in America? What happened to them later? Write your ideas in your notebook. Then share them with the class.

LEARNING STRATEGY

Reminder: When you identify what you already know about a topic, you are using the learning strategy **use what you know**. This strategy gets you ready to learn new information about the topic.

> *"Let it be recorded, that I am the last man of my people to lay down my gun."*
> — *Sitting Bull, 1890*

Treaties and Territories

"INDIAN TERRITORY"

In the 1830s, the U.S. government forced the Cherokees, the Sauk, and other Native American peoples to leave their eastern homelands and move west into "Indian Territory." At the time, this territory included land between the Missouri River and the Oregon Territory.

Many Native Americans had lived in this area for hundreds and hundreds of years. The Sioux, the Cheyenne, and the Arapaho were three groups who lived on the Great Plains. The Navajo, Apache, and Hopi people lived in the deserts of the Southwest.

THE MOVE TO RESERVATIONS

The U.S. government signed treaties, or written agreements, with the native peoples, promising that this land would belong to them "as long as the rivers shall run and the grass shall grow." However, in the second half of the 1800s, railroad owners, settlers, ranchers, and gold hunters all became very interested in this western land.

In the 1850s, the U.S. government began to buy parts of the Indian Territory from the native people and to move them to reservations, special land set aside by the government for Native

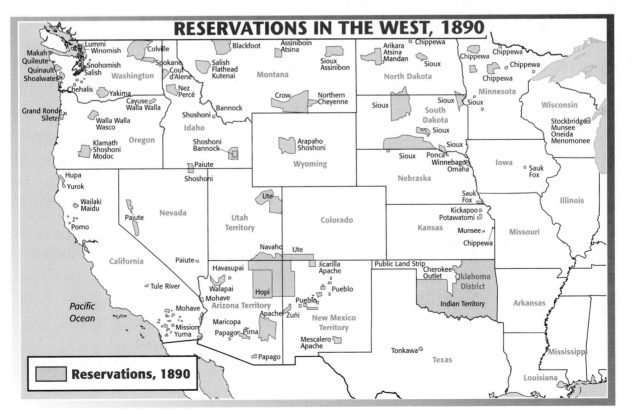

RESERVATIONS IN THE WEST, 1890

Reservations, 1890

Americans. Reservations were usually set up on land that white settlers didn't want. The native peoples were often forced to stay on these reservations.

Many native people did not want to sell their land. They did not want to live on reservations. They fought to save their homes, their hunting grounds, and their way of life.

The Native American people who lived on the Great Plains depended on the great buffalo herds for food, clothing, shelter, and tools. The settlers and railroad men killed millions of these buffalo for sport, for their fur, or to protect the new railroad tracks. In 1865, there were about 15 million buffalo on the Great Plains. Ten years later, only 1,000 buffalo were left.

The death of the buffalo meant the end of the way of life for the Native Americans of the Plains. There were terrible battles between the native peoples and U.S. soldiers. Thousands of Native Americans were killed. The remaining members of the tribes were moved to reservations.

Apache leader Geronimo and his wife

THE SIOUX NATION OF SOUTH DAKOTA

In 1874, gold was discovered in the Black Hills of South Dakota. The Black Hills belonged to the Sioux Nation. The U.S. government wanted to buy the land, but the Sioux did not want to sell. The U.S. Army was sent to fight the Sioux and to force them to leave the Black Hills and live on a reservation.

The Sioux fought the U.S. army. In 1876, led by Crazy Horse and Sitting Bull, the Sioux defeated General Custer and his forces in the Battle of Little Bighorn. This battle became known as Custer's Last Stand. General Custer and all his men were killed. After this battle, however, new U.S. forces fought the Sioux and defeated them. The Sioux were forced to move to a reservation. The Black Hills were taken over by gold miners and white settlers.

NATIVE AMERICANS OF THE SOUTHWEST DESERT

In the Southwest, Native Americans were also forced to move to reservations. Many Native Americans disliked reservation life and fought to live as they had in the past. One of the most famous fighters was Geronimo, leader of the Apache Nation. From 1876 to 1886, Geronimo and his Apache warriors attacked U.S. settlements and soldiers. Many men, women, and children—both Native American and settler—were killed before the Apache surrendered and returned to the reservation.

RESERVATION LIFE TODAY

Today, life on the reservations is not always easy, and many people are very poor. Some young people leave the reservations to live and work in the cities. Some reservations have set up businesses that make money to support the people who live on the reservation.

Many Native Americans still speak the language of their tribe. They believe it is important to keep the tribal culture alive. They want their children to remember and appreciate the way of life of their people. Native peoples have also been active in all professions, in government, sports, education, and the military.

UNDERSTANDING WHAT YOU READ Identifying What You Have Learned

Work with the same partner as in Before You Read (page 13). Discuss and take notes on the new information you have learned about Native Americans. Share what you have learned with the class.

Sitting Bull

LEARNING STRATEGY

While you listen, focus on the information you need to fill in the details and examples. This strategy is called **selective attention**. It helps you find specific information while listening or reading. Write down the information using key words and abbreviations only—not complete sentences. This strategy is called **taking notes**. It helps you remember information later and can be a good study guide. Together, these two strategies can help you become a better student!

Sioux leader Sitting Bull

Copy the T-list below into your notebook. Listen to some information about Sitting Bull, an important leader of the Sioux Nation. As you listen, take notes using the T-list. The main ideas are written on the left. Write the details and examples on the right. After you listen, compare your notes with two or three classmates. Did you forget anything? If so, add it to your notes. Finally, use your notes to write in your own words what you learned about Sitting Bull. Use complete sentences and paragraphs.

MAIN IDEAS	DETAILS AND EXAMPLES
A. Who was Sitting Bull?	_____ _____ _____ _____
B. Sitting Bull prepares the Sioux for battle (Custer's Last Stand)	_____ _____ _____ _____ _____ _____
C. After Custer's Last Stand	_____ _____ _____ _____
D. How Sitting Bull died	_____ _____ _____
E. Why Sitting Bull is important	_____ _____

The Desert Regions

The largest Native American reservation in the United States is the Navajo reservation that extends into parts of Arizona, New Mexico, and Utah. This reservation is in the Desert Region of the southwestern United States. The Hopi, Apache, and Zuni Nations also have reservations in the southwestern Desert Region.

Desert Regions are the driest regions on Earth. It is difficult for plants to grow and for people and animals to live in Desert Regions because little rain falls there.

Plants that do grow in deserts have special ways to get water. Some desert plants have long roots that go deep into the ground to find water. Other desert plants, such as the cactus, store water in their leaves so that they can survive when there is no rain.

The highest temperatures in the world are in Desert Regions. In the daytime, deserts are usually very hot. The sun shines brightly, there are few clouds, and there are no large trees to give shade. Deserts can also be very cold at night. The desert air is very dry, so the heat of the day disappears when the sun goes down.

In some deserts, people have made irrigation systems that bring water from far away. In Arizona and New Mexico, for example, there are many dams on rivers. Water collects behind the dams. This water is then delivered to desert areas so that farmers can grow crops.

Although deserts do not have much water, they do have other natural resources. The world's richest oil fields are in desert areas. In Desert Regions of the southwestern part of the United States, there are minerals such as copper, gold, silver, and uranium.

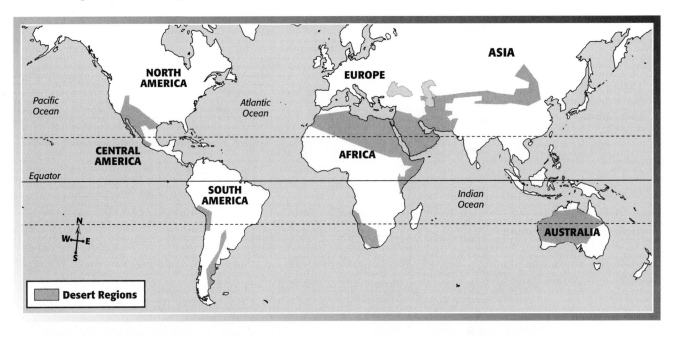

UNDERSTANDING WHAT YOU READ Using Maps for Comprehension

Look at the map of Desert Regions and answer these questions in your notebook.

1. Where is the largest Desert Region in the world?

2. Which continent in the map does not have a Desert Region?

3. In what part of the United States are Desert Regions found?

When you work in a group, you can learn new things from others. You also learn how to work with others. This learning strategy is called **cooperation**.

LEARNING STRATEGY

Could you live in a desert?

1. Think of things you would need in a desert. (If you live in a Desert Region, you already know a lot about the desert.) In your notebook, write a list of the ten most important things you would need to live in a desert.

2. Now sit in a group with four or five classmates. Compare your lists. Talk about the reasons why you chose each thing on your list. Listen to your classmates. Add to your list two good ideas that your classmates had.

3. With your classmates, talk about the five most important things that you would need to live in the desert. Talk about this until everyone in your group agrees on five important things. Then write these five things in a paragraph in your notebook by completing the sentences below. Give a good reason why each thing is necessary.

    _____ is important because _____. Do not forget to take _____ to the desert because _____. If you want to _____, you should take _____ to the desert. My group thinks that it is important to have _____ in the desert because _____. Finally, don't ever forget to take _____ to the desert because _____.

Monument Valley, located on the Navajo Reservation in northeastern Arizona

BEFORE YOU READ | **Identifying What You Already Know**

LEARNING STRATEGY

Reminder: Thinking, talking, or writing about what you know about a topic gets you ready to learn more about that topic. This learning strategy is called **use what you know**. Use it before you read or listen to new material.

Look at the names of inventions in the chart below. In your notebook, write a sentence that tells what you know about them.

Now read the rest of the information in the chart and be sure you understand how each invention is used. All these inventions were made in the United States. There were also important inventions in other countries.

Inventions in the United States: 1792–1903

DATE	INVENTION	INVENTOR	EXPLANATION
1792	Cotton gin	Eli Whitney	Takes seeds out of cotton. One person operating a cotton gin could do same work as fifty people picking seeds out by hand. Farmers could produce more cotton.
1834	Reaper	Cyrus McCormick	Horse-drawn machine cuts grain, such as wheat. Farmers in West could plant more wheat.
1844	Telegraph	Samuel F.B. Morse	Sends messages through wires, using a code for each letter of the alphabet. By 1850s, telegraph wires were all over United States. People could communicate over long distances quickly.
1846	Sewing machine	Elias Howe	Sews faster than by hand. Helped people to make clothes for their families more rapidly. Led to factories that made clothes (including uniforms for soldiers and sailors).
1856	Bessemer process	Henry Bessemer	Process for making stronger steel. Made it easier to create steel for railroads and machines.
1867	Typewriter	Christopher L. Sholes	Prints words faster than writing by hand. Changed the way people in offices worked. Many women found office jobs as typists.
1874	Barbed wire	Joseph Glidden	Fences in large farms in the prairie. Machine-made wire was cheap to buy. It ended the cattle drives.

1876	Telephone	Alexander Graham Bell	Sends spoken messages through wires. People could communicate by voice over long distances.
1877	Phonograph (record player)	Thomas A. Edison	Makes a permanent record of sounds. People could hear music and speech that had been played, sung, or spoken earlier, and they could hear it as often as they wished to.
1879	Electric lightbulb	Thomas A. Edison	Makes light using electricity. People could use electric lightbulbs in their homes instead of candles, gas lights, or oil lamps. Electricity made possible more light and was clean.
1888	Kodak camera	George Eastman	Takes a photograph. First simple camera that anyone could use. People could take pictures of family, friends, pets, etc.
1903	Airplane	Wilbur and Orville Wright	Transports people and things through the air. First flight of powered airplane at Kitty Hawk, North Carolina, December 17, 1903. Made travel much faster.

UNDERSTANDING WHAT YOU READ Study Questions

1. Write five questions about inventions in the United States in your notebook. Use the question words *when*, *what*, *who*, and *why*. Here are some examples of questions:

   When was the telephone invented?

   Who invented the telegraph?

   Why was the cotton gin important?

   What does the graph tell you about U.S. patents?

2. Now sit in groups of four or five. Take turns asking questions to the people in your group. When all the questions have been asked and answered, discuss the questions. Which were easy? Which were difficult? Write the two most difficult questions and their answers in your notebook.

NUMBER OF U.S. PATENTS	
YEAR	AVERAGE NUMBER PER YEAR
1790–1811	77
1820–1830	535
1840–1849	646
1850–1859	2,525
1890–1900	23,496

HISTORY MYSTERY

How did people in the cities keep track of time?

BEFORE YOU READ **What Would You Do?**

Reminder: For this activity, you need to use the learning strategy **cooperation**.

If you were a millionaire and wanted to help poor people, what would you do? Who (besides your family and friends) would you help? Instead of giving money to poor people, what other things could you do to make their lives better? Discuss your ideas with one or more classmates, and work together to prepare a short oral report for the class.

Reforms and Reformers

FACTORY LIFE: FRANCIS CABOT LOWELL

Francis Cabot Lowell was one of the early factory owners in the United States. Lowell believed that factory work did not have to be unpleasant. In the 1830s, he built a city along the Merrimack River in Massachusetts. His city, called Lowell, had factories for making cloth, but it also had boarding houses where the workers could rent rooms. The city had schools and churches, too.

At first, Francis Cabot Lowell hired young women from the farms near his city. He paid them more than they could earn on the farm. They lived in the boarding houses and followed a strict schedule. Lowell encouraged the women to eat healthy food and to go to church on their one day off. The "Lowell Girls," as they were called, were famous all over the United States because they wrote stories about life in the mills.

"Up before day, at the clang of the bell—and out of the mill by the clang of the bell—into the mill, and at work, in obedience to that ding-dong of a bell— just as though we were so many living machines."

—*Anonymous,* Lowell Offering *magazine*

Later factory workers were not as lucky as the Lowell Girls. They were badly paid. They worked very long hours. The factories were noisy and unhealthy. Some workers walked out of the mills to protest the long hours and low pay. They did not win and had to go back to work or be fired. In 1874, Massachusetts finally passed a law that workers could not work longer than ten hours each day. More and more children worked in the factories, and they worked in the same bad conditions and for the same long hours as adults.

Merrimack Mills and boarding houses, Lowell, Massachusetts, 1840s

The mill workers' strict schedule was based on hours of daylight.

HELP FOR THE POOR: JANE ADDAMS

In the last part of the 1800s, many men and women tried to help factory workers and other poor people. We call these men and women *reformers* because of the reforms, or changes, they tried to make. One of these people was Jane Addams.

Jane Addams was born in 1860. Her family was rich, but she wanted to help poor people. She traveled to London and visited a *settlement house*, a place where poor children could play and learn. In 1889, she started a settlement house in a poor neighborhood in Chicago. She called it Hull House. There she held classes in art, music, and crafts. She helped people learn to read better. Hull House took care of children during the days, and had a gymnasium where people could exercise. It also helped immigrants learn about the United States and prepare to become citizens.

WORDS AND PICTURES: JACOB RIIS

Jacob Riis helped the poor in a different way. He was born in Denmark and came to America as a young man. He found life as an immigrant in New York City hard. Work was not easy to find. Finally, he got a job as a police reporter on a newspaper.

Riis was always interested in the lives of the poor. In 1890, he wrote a book called *How the*

In 1900, more than one out of every six children in the United States worked in a factory or mine. This young girl worked in a textile factory.

Other Half Lives. In it, he told about life in the tenements, or apartment houses for the poor. He also took photographs of these apartments and of the people who lived in them. His books and pictures made people realize what life was like for poor people in the cities.

OTHER REFORMS: LAWS

Other reforms included laws to make factories safer and cleaner in many states. Other laws made sure that food was pure. Many states also passed laws to stop, or at least to limit, the hiring of children. Today, children are allowed to do farm work or to work for their parents, but they no longer can work in factories.

Necktie workshop in New York City, 1889

UNDERSTANDING WHAT YOU READ **Writing a Summary**

Reminder: When you **summarize**, you tell the main ideas in a reading in your own words. This strategy helps you check how well you have understood a reading.

LEARNING STRATEGY

In your notebook, write one or two sentences that tell the main ideas for each section of the reading Reforms and Reformers. Be sure to link your sentences so that they form a good paragraph. For instance, after writing about Lowell, you could write, "Another important reformer was Jane Addams."

Read your summary to a classmate and ask for feedback. Then revise and edit your summary.

The Statue of Liberty in New York harbor, the symbol of America for many immigrants

BEFORE YOU READ **Using Headings**

Look at the four headings in the reading on pages 23–24. Then read the questions below. Under which heading do you think you will find the answer to each question? In your notebook, write the name of the heading. Then scan to find the answer to the question. Write the answer under the heading in your notebook.

Reminder: When you scan a reading, you are looking for specific information. This learning strategy is **selective attention**. You can use it for reading and also for listening.

LEARNING STRATEGY

"Give me your tired, your poor, your huddled masses yearning to breathe free, The wretched refuse of your teeming shore. Send these, the homeless, tempest-tost to me, I lift my lamp beside the golden door!"
—Emma Lazarus, 1883

These lines are engraved at the foot of the Statue of Liberty.

1. Where did most immigrants in the 1700s come from?

2. When did the first English classes for immigrants start in public schools?

3. Are all Americans from immigrant families?

4. What kinds of jobs did U.S. immigrants get?

Now read the story to find out more information about immigrants in the United States.

Immigration to the United States

A NATION OF IMMIGRANTS

Immigrants are people who come into a new country to settle and live. The United States has always been a nation of immigrants. Except for Native Americans, everyone's family has come to the United States from another country at some time during the last three or four hundred years. Even the native peoples immigrated to the Americas from Asia many thousands of years ago.

Immigrant families wait in line at the Ellis Island processing center, 1900

Italian immigrants on a ferry to Ellis Island, 1905

Jewish immigrants, Ellis Island

EARLY IMMIGRANTS

In the 1600s and early 1700s, most immigrants came from Europe. Settlers immigrated to what is now the southwestern part of the United States from Spain. Other immigrants from England and other northern and western European countries settled on the east coast of North America. These east-coast people fought for independence from England. They helped build the new nation, the United States of America.

After the Civil War, many more people immigrated to the United States. There were three main reasons why so many immigrants came in the late 1800s. First, many people wanted religious freedom, just like the earlier immigrants to Plymouth, Massachusetts, in 1620. Second, many people wanted to live in a democratic country so that they could have

political freedom. Third, when crops in their native country were bad and there was not enough food, people came to the United States to have a better life.

HOW IMMIGRANTS SURVIVED

Life in the United States was not easy for most immigrants. Many immigrants were well educated in their own language, but they did not know English. Other immigrants had very little education and few skills. They all had to find jobs in order to survive. Immigrants from Europe entered through Ellis Island in New York City. Immigrants from Germany, Norway, and Sweden settled on the Great Plains and became farmers and business people. Thousands of immigrants came from Ireland, Italy, Russia, Poland, and other countries in southern and eastern Europe. They settled in large cities in the Northeast and worked in factories.

Chinatown, San Francisco

Many Chinese and Japanese immigrants arrived in California. They entered through Angel Island in San Francisco. They helped to build railroads and bridges in the western part of the country. Later, many Chinese and Japanese immigrants became farm workers or business owners.

English class for immigrants in New York City, 1910

IMMIGRANTS AND PUBLIC SCHOOLS

Public schools in the United States helped immigrants in many ways. First, the schools gave children a free education. This meant that many young people became better educated than their parents and had more chances for better jobs. In addition, many schools had evening classes for adults.

One of the important jobs of the schools was to teach English. At first, schools put immigrant children in classes with much younger English-speaking children until the immigrant children learned English. Some schools had bilingual classes in which students could study in their first language as well as in English.

In 1904, some schools started special language classes for children who did not speak English. Some companies also had classes in English for their workers. Today there are bilingual classes and ESL (English as a Second Language) or ESOL (English as a Second or Other Language) classes in many public schools.

Most of today's immigrants have the same kinds of difficulties in finding jobs and getting an education that earlier immigrants had. Like these earlier immigrants, today's immigrants hope that they can make a better life for themselves and their children.

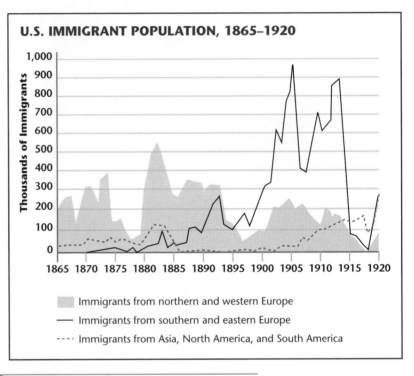

U.S. IMMIGRANT POPULATION, 1865–1920

y-axis: Thousands of Immigrants (0 to 1,000)
x-axis: 1865 1870 1875 1880 1885 1890 1895 1900 1905 1910 1915 1920

▢ Immigrants from northern and western Europe
— Immigrants from southern and eastern Europe
---- Immigrants from Asia, North America, and South America

UNDERSTANDING WHAT YOU READ **Comparing and Contrasting**

Work with a classmate. Draw a Venn diagram in your notebook. Label it *1. Why Immigrants Come to the U.S.* Draw a second Venn diagram and label it *2. How Immigrants Survive.* Then draw a third Venn Diagram and label it *3. Immigrants and Public Schools.* Label the left outer section of each Venn diagram *In the Past.* Label the right outer section *Now.*

Reread the text with your classmate. On the left (In the Past) of each diagram, write notes using the information in the text. On the right (Now) of each diagram, write what you know about immigrants today.

Compare the left and right sides of each Venn diagram. What is similar? Write these similarities in the middle section of the Venn diagram. Share with the class your Venn diagrams that compare and contrast immigration yesterday and today.

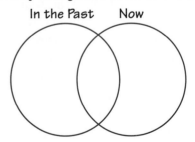

1. Why Immigrants Come to the U.S.

In the Past   Now

1. Work with a partner. For each part of the reading on pages 23–24, write one or two questions that will help you study and remember the main information in that section. Write your questions on a separate sheet of paper.

2. With your partner, write answers to your study questions on a second sheet of paper. Keep this answer key.

3. Now exchange your questions with another pair of students. They have to write answers to your questions—and you and your partner have to write answers to their questions!

4. Correct the answers that other students wrote for your questions using the answers you wrote on the second sheet of paper. They will also correct your answers.

5. Compare the results. Did either pair of students answer all the questions correctly?

DEVELOPING REPORTS **Immigrants**

Everyone in the United States originally comes from an immigrant family. Even Native Americans were immigrants many thousands of years ago. Many immigrants came from Europe a long time ago. Other people are more recent immigrants.

Many immigrants have made important contributions to the United States. Industrialist and philanthropist Andrew Carnegie, physicist Albert Einstein, and architect I. M. Pei were all immigrants to the United States. More recently, athletes like Monica Seles and the Alomar brothers (Sandy and Roberto) are immigrants who have become very well known in their new country.

Your teacher will help you select an important immigrant for research and report writing.

LEARNING STRATEGY

When you look for information in dictionaries, encyclopedias, atlases, biographies, the Internet, and other reference materials, you are using an important learning strategy. It is called **using resources**. Using resources is a good strategy when you need more information than what you can find in your textbook.

1. Look for information about the important immigrant you have chosen. You may want to use biographies, an encyclopedia, and the Internet.

2. As you read, take notes on the important information about the person. Write your notes on index cards. Use a new card for each source. Use your own words except when noting quotations that you think are important. Write the name of the author of that book or article and the date of publication in parentheses. Be sure to find the following information: complete name, date of birth, place of birth, when the person immigrated to the United States and why (if known), early years and education, occupation, accomplishments, major contributions (why this person is important in U.S. history).

3. Look over your note cards. Do you need any more information?

WRITING A FIRST DRAFT **Putting the Information Together**

1. Use your note cards to make an outline of your report. Complete the outline form below in your notebook. Add more items if necessary.

> ### [TITLE OF REPORT]
>
> **I.** Introduction
>
> Tell what your report will be about. Give the name and first nationality of your immigrant, and state why he or she is important.
>
> **II.** Early Life
>
> A. Date of birth and family background
> B. Education before the family immigrated to the United States
>
> **III.** Arrival in the United States
>
> A. Information about the family's reasons for emigrating (leaving), how they traveled, and any hardships they suffered
> B. Any information about arrival in the United States and the first days or weeks in the country
> C. Problems the person or his or her family had
>
> **IV.** Life in the United States
>
> A. Further education (if any)
> B. First job and subsequent jobs
> C. Marriage, children
> D. Accomplishments
>
> **V.** Conclusion
>
> Tell what your report was about by giving a brief summary of the important facts. Then tell why your immigrant is important in U.S. history.

2. When you complete your outline, you are ready to begin writing the first draft of your report. If possible, use a computer. This makes it easier to make revisions later.

REVISING Checking the Information in the Report

1. Read through your report. Does it have all the important information about your immigrant? Add anything that is missing.

2. Read through your report again. Have you repeated any information? Is there information that is not important to the biography of your immigrant? If so, take it out.

3. Now read your report out loud to a classmate. Is there something interesting you forgot to say? Ask for feedback. Take notes!

4. Now listen to your classmate's report. Give feedback that is helpful. If you are curious about something in your classmate's report, ask questions.

LEARNING STRATEGY

Reminder: When you work with someone else, you can learn more. This strategy is called **cooperation**.

EDITING Checking Spelling, Punctuation, and Grammar

1. Carefully check the spelling in your report. If you are using a computer, use the spell-check feature. Then reread carefully—the spell-check feature will not correct all errors! Correct all spelling mistakes. Use a dictionary if necessary.

2. Now check for punctuation and capitalization. Does every sentence start with a capital letter? Do all names of places and people start with capital letters? Do all sentences end with a period, a question mark, or an exclamation mark? Are there commas between clauses? Did you use quotation marks before and after quotes? Did you indent each paragraph? Correct any errors.

3. Now check the grammar. Remember to check the following:
    * Present tense, third-person singular ends in "-s" (she say<u>s</u>)
    * Adjectives come before nouns (a <u>poor</u> family)
    * Most verbs in a biography will be in the past tense (They <u>came</u> to the United States when she was ten years old.)

    Check with your teacher if you are not sure about grammar.

4. Read your report one last time. Are you satisfied? Is it the best work you can do? If so, turn it in to your teacher.

PRESENTING AN ORAL REPORT

Sit in a small group with three other classmates. Read your reports to each other. Be ready to answer questions after reading your report. In your notebook, write three important things that you learned from listening to each classmate's report.

Nine Presidents: 1865–1900

Nine men served as president of the United States between 1865 and 1900. Listed below are some things that happened while each was president.

	PRESIDENT	EVENTS
1865	Abraham Lincoln	1865 – Civil War ends; Lincoln killed
	Andrew Johnson	13th Amendment abolishes slavery
		1867 – United States buys Alaska from Russia for $7,200,000
		1868 – 14th Amendment gives citizenship to blacks
		Congress tries to remove President Johnson, fails by one vote
	Ulysses S. Grant	1869 – Wyoming gives vote to women
		Transcontinental railroad completed
1870		1870 – 15th Amendment guarantees voting rights for African American men
		1872 – Vice president Colfax accused of corruption
		1873 – *The Gilded Age,* by Mark Twain and Charles Warner, published
1875		
		1876 – General Custer attacks Sioux in Montana; he and 264 soldiers killed
		First telephone lines between cities
	Rutherford B. Hayes	1877 – Thomas A. Edison invents phonograph (record player)
		1879 – Thomas A. Edison invents electric lightbulb
1880		
	James A. Garfield (Mar. 4)	1881 – President Garfield shot July 2, dies September 19
	Chester A. Arthur (Sept. 20)	
		1882 – Chinese Exclusion Act forbids immigration of Chinese
		1883 – Congress sets up system of written tests for government jobs
1885	Grover Cleveland	
		1886 – American Federation of Labor (AFL) founded by Samuel Gompers
		1887 – Statue of Liberty completed in New York Harbor
	Benjamin Harrison	1889 – Jane Addams opens Hull House in Chicago
1890		1890 – Sherman Antitrust Act to regulate big businesses
		Jacob Riis publishes *How the Other Half Lives*
	Grover Cleveland	
		1894 – First showing of motion pictures (movies)
1895		
	William McKinley	
		1898 – Spanish-American War: United States acquires Puerto Rico, Guam, Philippines
		United States annexes independent republic of Hawaii
1900		

Ulysses S. Grant

Grover Cleveland

William McKinley

Use the time line on page 28 to answer these questions in your notebook.

1. The Constitution says that if a president dies during the term of office, the vice president becomes president. What two vice presidents became president in this way between 1865 and 1900, and when did they become president?

2. Which president served less than one year?

3. What happened in the same year that the transcontinental railroad was completed?

4. Which came first, the telephone or the electric lightbulb?

5. Many presidents have served two terms, but only one served two terms that did not immediately follow each other. Who was this president?

6. Under what president was a system of written tests set up for government jobs?

7. Who was president when the United States acquired Alaska?

8. Who owned Alaska before the United States bought it?

9. Impeachment by Congress is the first step in legally removing a president. Who is the only president impeached between 1865 and 1900?

10. Who was president when the United States went to war against Spain?

What do you think?

Imagine it is 1899. You live on a farm. You have just learned that your area is going to get electricity and telephone service next year. You've never seen electric lights or telephones, but you have read about them in newspapers and magazines.

Talk with a group of friends. How do you think these new inventions will change your life? Write your ideas in your notebook.

UNIT 2

Starting a New Century: 1900–1940

Tell what you think

Look at the images on these two pages. They describe events and inventions that happened just before and at the beginning of the twentieth century. What do you know about them? Why do you think these events and inventions were important?

Write your ideas in your notebook.

In this unit you will

- read about mass production and new inventions

- learn about World War I

- learn how different groups in the United States changed the way they lived

- find out about the Roaring Twenties, the Jazz Age, and the Great Depression

- find out and write about important men and women in music, medicine, and war

- use maps, charts, and graphs

- use photographs to tell a story about life in another time

- sharpen your listening, speaking, and note-taking skills

- find out how cartoons can tell a story

TIME LINE   1900   1905   1910

1913
16th Amendment

1913
17th Amendment

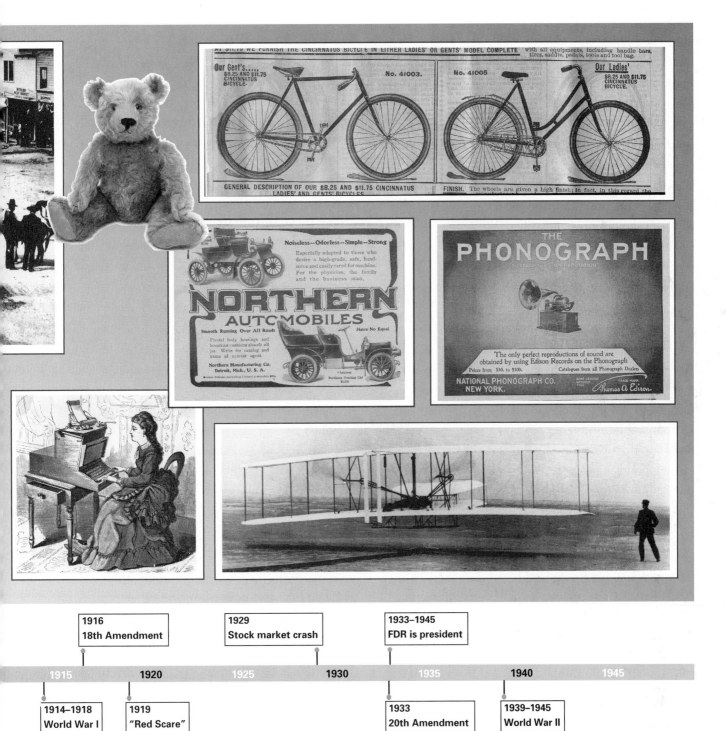

1916
18th Amendment

1929
Stock market crash

1933–1945
FDR is president

1915   1920   1925   1930   1935   1940   1945

1914–1918
World War I

1919
"Red Scare"

1933
20th Amendment

1939–1945
World War II

Write the words on the left below in your notebook. Then write the correct definition (from the right) next to each word or phrase.

1. to assemble

2. garment

3. goods

4. interchangeable part

5. mass production

6. optimistic

7. switchboard operator

8. trolley car

a. feeling good about your life and the future

b. a worker for the telephone company who connects the telephone calls

c. to put together

d. the manufacture of goods in large quantities

e. an electric streetcar that runs on tracks

f. things that are sold; products

g. a piece of clothing—like a shirt or a dress

h. a piece of one machine that can be used in place of the matching piece of another machine

LEARNING STRATEGY

Reminder: Look at each new word again. Draw or make a mental picture of each word. This strategy is called **using imagery**. It is a good way to remember items.

A New Era

There were many celebrations at the beginning of the twentieth century. Many citizens felt that the United States had overcome many difficulties to become a strong nation. The United States had added territory after a war with Spain and had purchased land from Russia. Factories were growing in cities, and many more products were being made by machine. Immigrants had continued to come to the United States, and this increased the population in the cities. People in the United States were generally optimistic.

For the next forty years, the United States would continue to grow and change. New

inventions would affect people's daily lives. The United States would become more involved in wars outside its borders, including in Asia, Latin America, and Europe. It would make laws that would affect many different groups, including women, blacks, Native Americans, and new immigrants.

THEODORE ROOSEVELT BECOMES PRESIDENT

President McKinley was assassinated in 1901, just a few months after he started his second term as president. His vice president, Theodore Roosevelt, then became the next president of the United States at the age of forty-two. He was younger than any other president and served as president for nearly eight years. Roosevelt was a popular president. He was well educated, had traveled in Europe, had fought in the Spanish-American War, and had raised cattle in the West. He used the newspapers to let people know about his ideas for the country.

Theodore Roosevelt was the first president to use an automobile for official business.

His policies extended the territory and power of the United States in the Philippines, Cuba, Puerto Rico, and Latin America. He liked to quote a West African proverb: "Speak softly, but carry a big stick." This proverb expressed his idea that the United States was strong enough as a nation to be involved in other areas of the world, acting like a police officer to protect the countries of the Western Hemisphere. The nations of Latin America did not like this policy. They remembered that U.S. support of a rebellion in Colombia had led to Colombia losing the territory of Panama. Panama became a country, and now the United States owned the part of the country around the Panama Canal.

At home, Theodore Roosevelt was a reformer. He carried out the ideas of the Progressive movement by regulating big corporations, increasing the authority over interstate commerce by the federal government, and setting standards for food and drugs. Because he increased the conservation of public lands, he is remembered as the first public conservationist.

MASS PRODUCTION IS INTRODUCED

One of the biggest changes in the new century was the introduction of mass production. Before mass production, many everyday items were made by hand or in small shops, meaning that not many products could be made at one time, and they were expensive. By *mass producing*, items could be made more quickly and for less money.

Several changes in factories made mass production possible.

Henry Ford was a builder of automobiles in Detroit, Michigan. He was the first manufacturer to create the American system of mass production. He designed his cars to use interchangeable parts. This meant that all of the parts for his automobiles were made by machines that could be set so that each type of item would be exactly like all the others. He also arranged the factory so that the workers remained in one place and the parts they needed were delivered to them. No one person built an entire car but instead added one part or section.

Then, in 1913, Henry Ford added the process that made mass production really possible: the moving assembly line. In this system, a moving belt carried the frame of the car past each worker, who added the same part to each car as it passed. Smaller moving belts and slides also brought parts to the workers. It was now possible for the workers to build cars very quickly. By 1925, workers were putting together one automobile every fifteen minutes. Because his factory could now make so many cars, Ford lowered the price and many more people, including his own factory workers, could afford to buy them. His most famous car was called the Model T. By 1922, the price was as low as $295.

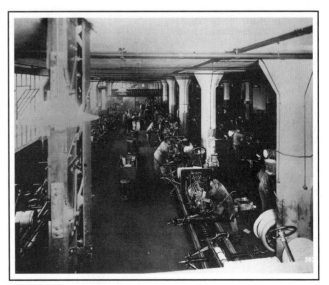

Assembly line, Ford Motor Company, 1914

After Henry Ford, most factories used mass production. Since more goods were being produced in this way, there were more things for people to buy. Because there were so many products, many companies began to advertise in local newspapers and in magazines. For example, the Sears, Roebuck catalogues became very popular. People could see a picture of each product for sale, a description, and the price. They could order and receive the product through the mail.

Automobiles became so popular, they caused traffic jams.

LIFE CHANGES WITH MASS PRODUCTION

Mass production changed people's lives. Men and women could buy some of their clothes, rather than having to make all of them at home. People could buy appliances such as washing machines, sewing machines, and vacuum cleaners, and this made life at home much easier. More and more houses in the cities could afford to have electricity.

A telephone company switchboard operator, 1922

Work days were different in the cities, where people worked by clock time, not by when the sun rose and set as they had done on the farms. People in cities would go to work on trolley cars instead of walking to work, so they did not have to live very close to their factory or office jobs. Some people drove cars to work.

Women who moved to the cities did not just work in factories. New migrants and immigrants often worked in the homes of others and did the cleaning, cooking, and caring for the children of their employers. Others did *piece work*. This meant that they went to a factory, picked up pieces of a garment, put them together at home, and then took the finished garment back to the factory. In poor families, even children did piece work. A few women also began to work at the telephone company as switchboard operators or in offices as typists.

UNDERSTANDING WHAT YOU READ | **Changes in Everyday Life**

Work with one or two classmates. Discuss the following questions. Then write your answers in your notebook.

1. What changes in the United States did Theodore Roosevelt make? Why do you think most people liked him? Give at least three reasons.

2. Mass production began about 100 years ago. What things do you use today that are mass produced?

3. In your own words, write a paragraph explaining how people's lives were easier because of mass production.

4. What changes affected the lives of women? How?

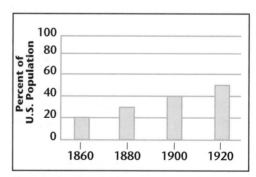
After the Civil War, more and more Americans moved to the cities.

BEFORE YOU READ | Tell What You Know

Work in a group with two or three classmates. What do you already know about labor unions? Do you know anyone who is a member of a labor union? What is the name of the union? What does the union do? Write your ideas in your notebook. Be prepared to share your group's ideas with the class.

Union logo

Workers' Power Grows

At first, factory owners made all of the rules about how long and how fast a worker had to work and about how much the worker was paid. Many owners were more interested in making money than in making sure the workers were safe. Before 1900, some factory workers in New England had threatened to quit if they did not get better working conditions. But because it was worse to be without a job than to work in bad conditions, most workers stayed even if the jobs were unhealthy or dangerous.

In the years between 1900 and 1915, more workers joined unions to try to make their work lives better. Groups of workers who made the same product (for example, clothes) or did the same job (such as make cars or steel) could all threaten to strike, or stop working, if the factory owner did not make changes. If many workers from the same factory left, the owner would lose money. The unions believed that threatening to walk out would make factory owners treat them better.

Sometimes things changed because workers were hurt or killed. In 1911, there was a terrible fire at the Triangle Shirtwaist factory in New York City. The unsafe conditions of the factory caused the fire to spread, and many people, mostly women, were trapped in the factory and died. After that fire, new unions began to ask for changes in working conditions. Several of the unions formed at that time, such as the American Federation of Labor (AFL) and the International Ladies' Garment Workers' Union (ILGWU), still exist today as part of larger unions.

Firefighters extinguish the fire at the Triangle Shirtwaist factory

UNDERSTANDING WHAT YOU READ | Using Context

LEARNING
STRATEGY

Reminder: When you see a new word, you can often figure out its meaning with the strategy **making inferences**. Look at the words before and after the new word. They will help you make a good guess.

Reread the selection about labor unions. Use the context to make inferences about the meanings of the words below. Write your guesses in your notebook.

| join | conditions | threaten | unsafe |

Now check these words in the Glossary. How many correct inferences did you make using context? If your inference was not correct, write the correct meaning in your notebook.

BEFORE YOU READ **Identifying What You Already Know**

Work with a classmate. What have you already learned about the history of immigration to the United States? Write what you know in your notebook. Share the information with the class.

LEARNING STRATEGY

Reminder: Learning new information is easier if you think about what you already know about a topic. This gets you ready to learn more about the same topic. This learning strategy is called **use what you know**.

New Opportunities

NEW IMMIGRANTS

Immigrants looking for better lives continued to come to the United States in the late nineteenth and early twentieth centuries. The cities began to grow quickly as new immigrants settled there. The cities became more and more crowded. Immigrants to the cities wanted to learn about their new country, but they did not want to forget their old countries. So new immigrants often settled in neighborhoods where people from their native country or region were already living. In these ethnic neighborhoods, immigrants from the same country could speak their native language, eat familiar food, and follow the customs and religions of their native country. They could help each other until they were able to move to better places.

Tenements in lower Manhattan, New York, early 1900s

The Vanderbilt mansion on Fifth Avenue, New York, 1908

Immigrants from Eastern Europe came into the United States through Ellis Island in New York City. Many from Asian countries, however, entered the United States through Angel Island on the West Coast. Chinese immigrants had come to the United States in the 1800s to search for gold and later to work on the railroads. They were mostly men without families who planned to earn money and then return to China. In 1882, the U.S. government passed a law called the Chinese Exclusion Act to keep more Chinese people from coming to the United States. New immigrants from Japan also came to the United States. They often brought wives and families because they intended to stay in the United States and farm. After 1900, Japanese, some Chinese, and many Mexican immigrants continued to enter the United States.

THE GREAT MIGRATION

Not everyone who moved to cities at the beginning of the twentieth century was an immigrant. Some people moved from other parts of the United States because they wanted better jobs. The growing number of factories in cities in the North meant more jobs. The chance to make more money working in a factory encouraged an ever-growing number of people to migrate to the cities from the farms.

The movement of large numbers of African Americans from the poor farms of the South to find work in the factories of the North was called the Great Migration. It began about 1915 and lasted until about 1940. In that time more than 1 million people moved from the South to the North. There were several reasons why so many African Americans moved to the North. First, an insect (the boll weevil) began to thin the cotton crops, and poor farmers could not make enough money to live. Second, people who had already gone to the North wrote to friends and family in the South to tell them that there were jobs and better schools in the North. Third, some of the laws in the South after the Civil War and Reconstruction made life very difficult for African Americans. Some white people terrorized African Americans, hurting and even killing some people.

In the North, African Americans concentrated in the city neighborhoods and began to build cultural and political power. They opened businesses, published newspapers, and created art and music. African Americans had more opportunities there to work in politics and many other professions. You will read later about some of the talented African Americans who brought ideas, music, and art to the American experience in the 1920s and beyond.

Leaving the South, headed north

UNDERSTANDING WHAT YOU READ **Comparing and Contrasting**

Look at the image and the text on this page. Work with a classmate to discuss the questions below. Write your answers in your notebook.

1. What caused African American farmers to leave the South?

2. Why were they attracted to the North?

Now discuss with your classmate and write down what each of you knows about immigration.

3. What causes immigrants to leave their countries?

4. Why are immigrants attracted to the United States today?

Construct a graphic organizer that compares and contrasts reasons for the Great Migration and reasons for immigration from other countries today.

Read the definitions below. Then skim through the next reading to find the underlined words that match the definitions. Write the words and definitions in your notebook.

1. making mechanical drawings

2. hurt or wounded

3. a contract that pays for medical help for workers

4. reporters or writers for a newspaper

5. people who make laws

6. people or groups that work to improve the lives of others

7. the farms, not the cities

8. the cities, not the farms

9. related to an occupation such as secretary or mechanic

The Progressive Movement

Progressives were people who wanted to continue some of the reforms that had started at the end of the nineteenth century. They wanted to make life better for children, for immigrants, and for the poor. People in the Progressive movement were writers, journalists, legislators, educators—men and women, black and white. They all wanted to make the government work better for all people. They were most interested in the problems caused by the rapid growth of factories and the crowded cities. They worked with the government to make changes. The ideas of Progressives were published in books and in magazines, and many people discussed these ideas.

EDUCATION

In the early part of the twentieth century, education became an important part of the life of children in cities and on farms. Just after the Civil War, there were about 7 million children attending school, but by 1920, almost

A classroom in the South

21 million were in school. In <u>rural areas</u>, the one-room school was very common. In one-room schools, children of different ages were all in the same classroom, and one teacher had to teach everything. At first, schools only educated young children, but with more and more children in cities, schools expanded to educate high school–age children. In these <u>urban areas</u>, the schools had several rooms, and students were divided by grades. The schools taught reading and mathematics, and they also began to teach <u>vocational</u> subjects such as typing, <u>drafting</u>, and how to use tools. School leaders understood that students needed to learn these skills to get some of the new jobs of the new century.

NEW LAWS AND AMENDMENTS

Progressives worked to pass new laws. They succeeded in getting laws that required food inspection, established the eight-hour work day, made factories safer, and gave workers <u>insurance</u> to help pay medical costs if they were <u>injured</u> at work or became sick. Other laws made business practices fair to all, made cities more beautiful, and kept children in school instead of working in factories.

The importance of the Progressive movement was also found in four new amendments to the Constitution that were approved between 1913 and 1920. It is hard to

SOME LEADERS OF THE PROGRESSIVE MOVEMENT

Ida Tarbell

Jacob Riis

Upton Sinclair

amend the Constitution, so to have four changes in seven years was very unusual. One allowed the national government to collect income taxes from all working people. One prohibited the sale of alcohol, one gave women the right to vote, and the last one gave citizens the right to vote directly for the senators from their states.

UNDERSTANDING WHAT YOU READ | **Thinking about Effects**

Many new laws resulted from the ideas of the Progressive movement. Work with two or three classmates to discuss how these laws affected different people. Think about one or more of the following types of people: children, women, factory workers, other hourly workers, factory owners, teachers, people from rich and poor families. Make a chart that shows the type(s) of people, the new laws, and the effects these laws had on their lives. Hint: Think about people's lives before and after each new law.

LEARNING STRATEGY

Reminder: Using the learning strategy **cooperation** will help you complete this assignment by sharing all the ideas in your group.

Vocabulary

The next two readings are about World War I. Some of the important words in the two readings are listed below in the left column. Synonyms or short definitions are listed in the right column. Copy the fifteen vocabulary words in your notebook, and write the correct definition next to each one.

1. armistice	**a.** army or group of soldiers
2. assassinate	**b.** injury
3. czar	**c.** German undersea boat
4. fire on	**d.** stop participating
5. huge	**e.** solitary
6. lone	**f.** agreement to stop fighting
7. overthrow	**g.** staying out of a war
8. neutrality	**h.** shoot at
9. submarine	**i.** enormous; very large
10. survive	**j.** king
11. trench	**k.** murder by secret attack
12. troops	**l.** undersea boat or ship
13. U-boat	**m.** live on
14. withdraw	**n.** get rid of by force
15. wound	**o.** excavation or hole dug in the ground

Studying a Map

Study the map of Europe in 1914 at the beginning of World War I. Find these countries: *Britain, France, Italy,* and *Russia.* These countries were the *Allies* in World War I. Now find these countries: *Austria-Hungary* and *Germany.* These countries were the main *Central Powers* in World War I. In your notebook, make a list of both groups of countries. Find *Bosnia* and its capital, *Sarajevo.* Draw a circle around Sarajevo. This is where World War I started.

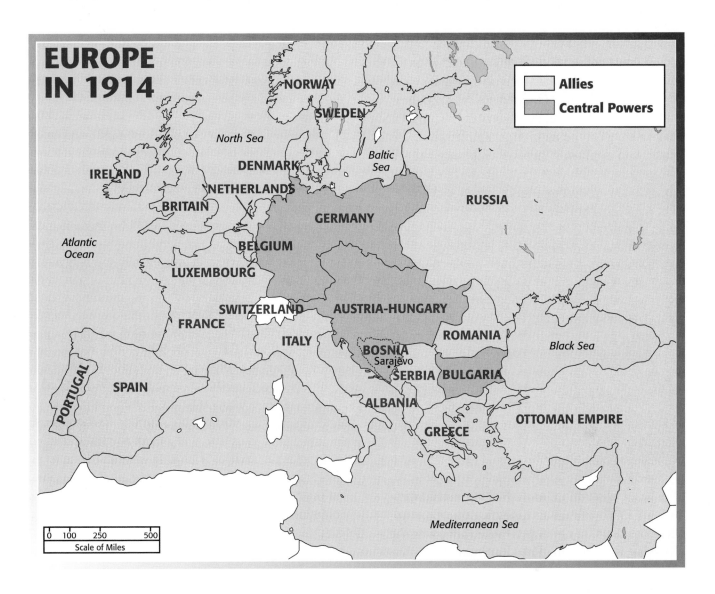

EUROPE IN 1914

Allies
Central Powers

NORWAY
SWEDEN
North Sea
Baltic Sea
IRELAND
DENMARK
NETHERLANDS
BRITAIN
GERMANY
RUSSIA
Atlantic Ocean
BELGIUM
LUXEMBOURG
SWITZERLAND
AUSTRIA-HUNGARY
FRANCE
ITALY
ROMANIA
BOSNIA
Sarajevo
Black Sea
SERBIA
BULGARIA
PORTUGAL
SPAIN
ALBANIA
OTTOMAN EMPIRE
GREECE
Mediterranean Sea

0 100   250   500
Scale of Miles

"The War to End All Wars"

EUROPE ENTERS WORLD WAR I

While factories and cities in the United States were growing, countries in Europe were entering a war. These countries had made secret agreements to defend each other if attacked, and some groups in Europe also wanted to form their own nations. Then the Archduke of Austria was assassinated in Bosnia in 1914. Since Germany had an agreement to help Austria, it declared war on Serbia because a Serbian had killed the Archduke. More and

more nations acted on their treaties and declared war on other countries, resulting in one of the worst wars in history, World War I. In 1914, there were two groups of countries fighting each other: The Central Powers (Austria-Hungary and Germany) fought against the Allies (Britain, France, Italy, and Russia).

The United States did not want to be involved in a war so far away, so it declared neutrality and hoped that the European countries could make peace.

The United States Enters World War I

Many people in the United States found it difficult to stay neutral in World War I. Products made in U.S. factories were traded with Britain, France, and Germany. Many U.S. citizens had come as immigrants from European countries that were fighting the war. Some people felt that the United States should support the country of their family's origin. Then a German U-boat sank the British ocean liner *Lusitania* in 1915. Of the nearly 1,200 people who died, more than 100 were Americans. This turned more people in the United States against Germany, but there were still many who wanted peace. For two more years, the United States provided supplies to the Allies and tried to remain isolated, or to stay apart and out of the war. But in early 1917, German submarines began to target American ships. The United States declared war on Germany in April 1917.

November 11 is still a day of remembrance in the United States. It is called Veterans' Day and honors all the Americans who have fought in wars for their country.

Just before the United States entered the war in 1917, there was a revolution in one of the countries on the Allies' side. This was the Russian Revolution. The Communists

HISTORY MYSTERY

"A lone assassin's bullet had plunged Europe into a war that would change history." What does the writer mean? Write your interpretation in your notebook.

(sometimes called "Reds"), led by Lenin, overthrew the czar of Russia and took over the government. Russia withdrew from the war, leaving the other nations to continue fighting.

When the United States finally entered the war, it had been going on for almost three years, and all the countries were exhausted from fighting. The entry of the United States into the war brought new soldiers and supplies to the Allies, and the war began to turn in the Allies' favor. It would still be a long struggle before the fighting finally ended at the eleventh hour of the eleventh day of the eleventh month in 1918 (11/11/18).

UNDERSTANDING WHAT YOU READ Making a Time Line

LEARNING STRATEGY

Reminder: A time line is a **graphic organizer** that shows a sequence of events. It helps you understand how things happened in the past.

Work with a classmate. In your notebook, make a time line of the events of World War I, beginning in 1914 and ending in 1918. You will need to find additional information about the events of the war and the people involved in it. In your notebook, write three places where you will look for more information.

When you have finished your time line, share it with the rest of the class.

You have probably seen images of today's wars and conflicts on television. World War I was fought before there was television, but there are photographs of that terrible war. Look carefully at the photographs. What things do you see that are similar to today's wars that we see on TV? What things are different?

In your notebook, write a paragraph that describes the similarities and differences between these images of World War I and today's wars.

Troops construct plank roads to allow heavy traffic to pass.

From a soldier's diary before the Battle of the Marne: "Trucks, artillery, infantry columns, cavalry, wagons, caissons, mud, MUD, utter confusion."

Battle in the air

French tanks and infantry going to the front

U.S. gunners defend French territory.

The War Experience

World War I was called the "Great War" and the "war to end all wars." However, it did not end all wars, and a large number of the young men who fought in it died.

The fighting in World War I was extremely difficult. There was fighting in the air for the first time in any war. Tanks, machine guns, and submarines were also used for the first time. The war was fought over the same areas of land many times. Soldiers dug trenches and had to stay in them for days or weeks at a time. Both sides used poison gas in the fight, and large numbers of soldiers died from infection, disease, and poison gas, as well as from bullets.

World War I saw many more soldiers wounded than in earlier wars, but it also saw the development of new ways of treating wounds and diseases. For example, for the first time, trained nurses worked on the battlefield. In addition, the newly developed medical technique of plastic surgery made it possible to repair many of the worst wounds. These and other improvements meant that soldiers had a better chance to survive.

WAR CASUALTIES

All of the countries involved in World War I lost many soldiers. Almost 4½ million Americans fought in this war, and 350,000 were wounded or died. The other countries that fought in this war lost even more people. Of the 12 million soldiers fighting for Russia, more than 9 million were killed, wounded, or missing. France had more than 6 million casualties; the British Empire more than 3 million. Germany had more than 7 million soldiers dead, wounded, or missing.

UNDERSTANDING WHAT YOU READ Reading a Table

Study the table. Then answer the questions in your notebook.

COUNTRIES	TOTAL MOBILIZED	KILLED & DEAD	WOUNDED	PRISONERS & MISSING	TOTAL CASUALTIES	CASUALTIES (% OF MOBILIZED)
Allied Powers						
Russia	12,000,000	1,700,000	4,950,000	2,500,000	9,150,000	76.3
France	8,410,000	1,357,800	4,266,000	537,000	6,160,800	76.3
British Empire	8,904,467	908,371	2,090,212	191,652	3,190,235	35.8
Italy	5,615,000	650,000	947,000	600,000	2,197,000	39.1
United States	4,355,000	126,000	234,300	4,500	364,800	8.2
Romania	750,000	335,706	120,000	80,000	535,706	71.4
Serbia	707,343	45,000	133,148	152,958	331,106	46.8
Montenegro	50,000	3,000	10,000	7,000	20,000	40.0
Japan	800,000	300	907	3	1,210	0.2
Belgium	267,000	13,716	44,686	34,659	93,061	34.9
Greece	230,000	5,000	21,000	1,000	17,000	11.7
Portugal	100,000	7,222	13,751	12,318	33,291	33.3
TOTAL	**42,188,810**	**5,152,115**	**12,831,004**	**4,121,090**	**22,104,209**	**52.3**
Central Powers						
Germany	11,000,000	1,773,700	4,216,058	1,152,800	7,142,558	64.9
Austria-Hungary	7,800,000	1,200,000	3,620,000	2,200,000	7,020,000	90.0
Turkey	2,850,000	325,000	400,000	250,000	975,000	34.2
Bulgaria	1,200,000	87,500	152,390	27,029	266,919	22.2
TOTAL	**22,850,000**	**3,386,200**	**8,388,488**	**3,629,829**	**15,404,477**	**67.4**

1. Which country lost the greatest number of soldiers fighting in the war?

2. Which country had the greatest number of injuries in proportion to the number of soldiers fighting in the war?

3. Which country had the greatest number of total casualties in proportion to the number mobilized?

4. Almost all of the soldiers who died in World War I were young men between the ages of 17 and 25. What changes do you predict might happen in a country after a war in which so many young men died? Write your predictions.

Europe changed after World War I. Look carefully again at the map of Europe in 1914 before World War I on page 41. Then study the map on this page, which shows Europe after World War I. What changed? What countries became larger? What countries became smaller? Why do you think this happened? Work with a classmate and write your ideas in your notebook. Share your ideas with the class.

EUROPE AFTER WORLD WAR I

New Countries

The Treaty of Versailles

THE TREATY AND THE FOURTEEN POINTS

U.S. President Woodrow Wilson wanted a peace treaty that would keep peace for a long time. He suggested that the treaty should include a number of ideas. These ideas became known as the Fourteen Points. Many of the points were about which countries would control the land where the war had been fought, and how nations would trade and make agreements.

The Treaty of Versailles (1919) included some of Wilson's ideas, along with those of the leaders of Britain and France. These countries wanted to punish Germany for starting the war, and they wanted to make sure that Germany would never be able to fight again. The treaty said that Germany would lose a great deal of land (see the map above) and weapons, and would have to pay for the damage caused by the war. Germany was unable to do this because the long war had made the country very poor. Nevertheless, as the loser in the war,

Germany was forced to sign the Treaty of Versailles.

THE LEAGUE OF NATIONS

President Wilson believed that the most important idea he had proposed for the Treaty of Versailles was the fourteenth point about the formation of an international organization of nations. These nations would meet together to settle disputes peacefully instead of by war. This organization was to be called the League of Nations. Although many people in the United States agreed with President Wilson, the Senate (the part of Congress that approves treaties) did not agree. The Senate refused to approve the treaty because its members believed that the United States should not get involved in international problems. All the European nations that had fought in World War I signed the Treaty of Versailles. The United States did not.

Reminder: When you **summarize**, you write down the important information in a reading in your own words.

LEARNING STRATEGY

Write a summary of the Treaty of Versailles in your notebook.

Using Headings

Look at the four headings in the next reading. Then read the questions below. Under which heading do you think you will find the answer to each question? Write the heading title in your notebook. Then scan to find the answer to the question. Write the answer underneath the heading in your notebook.

Reminder: Use the learning strategy **selective attention** when you are trying to find specific information in a reading. This strategy helps you scan a reading.

LEARNING STRATEGY

1. How many Mexican immigrants came to the United States between 1910 and 1920?

2. What dangers could African Americans encounter at this time?

3. What were some of the positive things that happened in this period?

4. Why were some people afraid of the Communists, or "Reds"?

Times of Contrast

At the time of World War I, there was a great deal of intolerance (the fear of something or someone who looks or thinks differently than you) in the United States. This was not new, because intolerance has had a long history in America. There have been people who have been intolerant toward Native Americans, abolitionists, African Americans, Catholics, union members, or supporters of women's rights. After World War I, however, these fears led to violence against certain groups.

THE RED SCARE

Many people were afraid of Russian Communists. When the Communists seized power in Russia in 1917, they had encouraged workers in other countries to also overthrow their own governments. Communists were called "Reds," and they were hated and feared by many people.

At this time in the United States, there were several big strikes by workers in Seattle, Boston, and Pittsburgh, and bombs were sent in the mail to some government officials. Some people thought this was done by communists and that members of labor unions were communists. In 1920, the government arrested many people suspected of being communists. In some cases, people's rights were denied and the law was not followed. This period of fear and suspicion was called the "Red Scare." It would reappear in the 1950s.

INTOLERANCE TOWARD AFRICAN AMERICANS

After World War I, there were attacks on African Americans in both the South and the North. A series of race riots left many people, both black and white, dead or homeless in northern cities. Lynch mobs also killed many African Americans in the North and the South. *Lynching*, the hanging or killing of a person by a mob, resulted in the deaths of hundreds of blacks in the years after World War I. The Ku Klux Klan (KKK), an organization of intolerant whites, often used lynching to frighten people they hated so that these people would leave an area or do what the Klan wanted. There were many people, however, who opposed lynching. Groups such as the National Association for the Advancement of Colored People (NAACP) and the Urban League, and individuals such as newspaper editor Ida B. Wells, worked hard to oppose the way that African Americans and others were being discriminated against or hurt and killed.

Ku Klux Klan members parade before a burning cross, 1920s

RESTRICTIVE IMMIGRATION LAWS

Immigrants continued to come to the United States, but in fewer numbers. Even with reduced numbers, however, the government did not always want to let in everyone who wanted to come here to live. Several laws were passed to limit the number of immigrants from certain countries. The Emergency Immigration Act in 1921 set a *quota*, or specific number, for people from countries in eastern and southern Europe and from Africa and Asia. (The immigration of people from China had already been stopped by an 1882 act.) But the laws did not stop immigration from Mexico. Between 1910 and 1920, about 170,000 people from Mexico entered the United States to fill jobs on farms in the Southwest and to escape war and poverty.

CHANGES FOR THE BETTER

Not all of the changes after World War I were bad ones. For many people, moving to the United States or migrating from rural areas to cities was good. People who moved to the cities made more money than they had on the farm. There was better education in the cities. Women won the right to vote across the nation when the 19th Amendment was added to the Constitution in 1920. Other ideas about government and business were also important to the rest of the world.

UNDERSTANDING WHAT YOU READ | **Working with Study Questions**

1. Work with a partner. For each section of the reading, write one or two questions that will help you study and remember the main information in that section. Write your questions on a sheet of paper.

2. With your partner, write answers to your study questions on a second sheet of paper. Keep this as your answer key.

3. Now exchange your questions with another pair of students. They have to write answers to your questions—and you and your partner have to write answers to their questions.

4. Now correct the answers that the other students have written for your questions using the answers you wrote in item 2. They will also correct your answers.

5. Compare the results. Which pair of students answered all the questions correctly?

Analyzing Images

Right after World War I, people were very tired of war and they wanted to have fun. Look at the pictures below. What things do you think people did to have a good time? Why? Work with a classmate and write your ideas in your notebook.

Famous hitter Babe Ruth at bat

Duke Ellington's Cotton Club Orchestra

Dancing the Charleston

Charles Lindbergh, first man to fly solo across the Atlantic

A woman urges others to vote

Satchel Paige, star of the Negro Baseball League

READING AND TAKING NOTES

LEARNING STRATEGY

Reminder: When you focus on the information you need, you are using the strategy **selective attention.** You need to pay selective attention in order to use another important learning strategy: **taking notes.** When you take notes on the most important information, you can use your notes to review the information later. Remember, write down key words only and abbreviations if possible.

You will read about both good things and bad things that happened in the 1920s. Make a T-list in your notebook. Label one column *Good things in the 1920s* and label the other column *Bad things in the 1920s.* Read "A Decade of Excess" and take notes as you read, writing events and situations in either the *Good things* or the *Bad things* column. After reading, compare your notes with two or three classmates. Did you agree on what was good or bad? Why or why not? In your notebook, explain why you agreed or disagreed with your classmates.

A Decade of Excess

The 1920s have been called many things—the Roaring Twenties, the Jazz Age, the Lawless Decade, and the Era of Wonderful Nonsense. People were happy that the war was over, and they wanted to enjoy life again.

People bought cars and traveled. They enjoyed going to fairs and watching airplane stunt pilots. Fashions changed and many young women, called flappers, cut their hair short and wore short dresses. A new dance called the Charleston was very popular, and so were dance marathons—dance contests in which couples danced as long as they could. The last couple standing won.

In addition to the fun and silliness of the Roaring Twenties, there were also changes that had important consequences and affected many people.

PROHIBITION AND GANGSTERS

In 1919, a new amendment had been passed that prohibited the manufacture, transportation, and sale of liquor (such as whiskey, gin, wine, and beer). Many believed that alcohol was a poison that ruined people's health and led to poverty. They also believed that the government could and should control personal choices people made. So the Prohibition amendment was approved, but it soon became obvious that it could not be enforced. Smugglers brought in liquor from Canada or from the Caribbean. Gangsters brought illegal liquor into the cities, where much of it was sold to *speakeasies*, or illegal restaurants or bars. Smuggling and selling illegal liquor was called bootlegging. Even though Prohibition agents tried to arrest people who were breaking the Prohibition law, they were often not successful. Some people tricked these government inspectors by smuggling bottles of liquor into parties under their big coats, in their baggy pants, or in the legs of their boots.

Bootlegging became a successful business for gangsters such as Al Capone and Dutch Schultz. The law did not stop liquor sales, and the Prohibition amendment was finally repealed in

First Prohibition Commissioner: "This law will be obeyed in cities large and small, and in villages, and where it is not obeyed it will be enforced. The law says that liquor to be used as a beverage must not be manufactured. We shall see that it is not manufactured. Nor sold, nor given away, nor hauled in anything on the surface of the earth or under the earth or in the air."

1933. But the gangsters also controlled other kinds of crime in the big cities. They became rich and powerful, and organized crime continued to be a problem in many cities.

THE HARLEM RENAISSANCE

During the 1920s, there was a creative outpouring by African American musicians, artists, and writers. One of the centers for this renaissance was New York City's Harlem neighborhood. In music, a new sound came from the South and was played by African American musicians, often in New York City speakeasies. This sound was called jazz, a kind of music made famous by great musicians such as "Jelly Roll" Morton, Duke Ellington, and Fletcher Henderson. This was the Jazz Age.

African Americans became famous in other arts as well. The poet Langston Hughes, the writer Zora Neale Hurston, and the singer-actor Paul Robeson are some of the other famous artists of this time. The Harlem Renaissance stands as a monument to African American cultural creativity.

ORDINARY LIFE IN THE 1920S

Not everyone's life included flappers, fast cars, and speakeasies. Many people went to movies and listened to the radio or read the new magazines like the *Saturday Evening Post* or *Reader's Digest*. Some enjoyed going to baseball games to watch famous players like Babe Ruth of the New York Yankees or Satchel Paige of the Negro League. For many, real wages rose by almost 20 percent, and life seemed much better.

But this would not last. The decade to follow would be a very difficult time.

Read the comic strip below and look for the vocabulary words. Try to figure out the meanings of these words from the context. (Some of these words are in the reading on "The Great Depression".) Write your guesses in your notebook.

share	lay off	speculation
stock market	investor	drought
broker	unemployed	bonus
loan	salary	shack
goods		

October 1929

Now work with a classmate and use the Glossary to check the meaning of the vocabulary words. Reread the comic strip to help you understand the meanings. Then write the definitions in your notebook.

Reminder: When **making inferences** about word meanings, you need to look at the whole context. This means looking at the sentences before and after the word and also looking at any illustrations that can help.

LEARNING
STRATEGY

The Great Depression

An economic depression is a time when businesses make fewer goods and pay their workers less, there is high unemployment, and people have little money to buy anything.

SPECULATION

In the 1920s, a lot of people had money to spend. Mass production had made goods less expensive, and workers earned higher salaries. Many people began to gamble on the fact that the stock market (where owners sold shares, or pieces, of their companies) would go up and they would make "easy" money. They bought on speculation. This meant that they paid part of the price of the share and borrowed the rest from a broker (or stockbroker). If the company earned money, then the speculator made money. If the company did not earn money or lost money, then the speculator owed the broker and lost the original investment. But a number of events changed everything.

DROUGHT IN THE MIDWEST

Farms in the Midwest were having problems with weather. A severe drought had made crop land turn to dust. Unusual winds—called the Dust Bowl storms—blew the good soil off the land and made the land useless for farming. Farmers in Oklahoma, Texas, and Kansas packed up their belongings and moved west to California, hoping to find new farmland. These moving farmers became known as "Okies." For farms that did have crops, the prices were so low that the farmers could not pay their loans and had to sell their farms. Between 1930 and 1934, almost 1 million farms were lost by their owners.

THE STOCK MARKET CRASH

All through American history, prices of shares have gone up and down. On October 29, 1929, however, prices went down but

People stand in line for relief supplies

they did not go back up. Prices on the stock market fell so low that most investors lost all their money. This day was called Black Tuesday, the day the stock market "crashed." People who had speculated had to pay back to the stockbroker what they had borrowed. After the crash, many people had very little money, so they could not buy any new products. Since people were not buying goods, the factories could not sell their products, and business was bad. Since business was bad, factories and other businesses began to lay off workers. Unemployment began to rise. Everyone felt very unsure about the future.

A Dust Bowl storm in a midwestern town, 1930s

Bonus Army

Some groups asked the government for help. In 1924, Congress had passed a bill to give World War I veterans a bonus to be paid out over twenty years. But by 1931, many veterans were struggling and without jobs. A Texan congressman suggested that a law be passed to pay out the money immediately. Over 20,000 veterans, called the "Bonus Army," came to Washington, DC, to support the law. It did not pass, and most of the veterans went home. But about 2,000 veterans and their families remained in Washington, living in cardboard and metal shacks and organizing protests. President Hoover ordered the U.S. Army to keep order, but instead they pushed the veterans and their families out and burned their shacks. Many people felt terrible about how the veterans had been treated. They waited to see what would happen next.

President Hoover and Congress Try to Recover

Many people in Congress wanted the national government to give money to help the workers and farmers who were suffering.

Acres of shacks housed the many poor people during the Depression.

Congress passed some laws to help make things better and get people back to work. President Hoover had a different idea. He did not want to give people money. He thought that people would help each other without the government's money. However, even people who wanted to help could not, because they did not even have enough money for their own families.

UNDERSTANDING WHAT YOU READ Identifying Cause and Effect

The story of how the United States went from prosperity in the Roaring Twenties to hardship in the Great Depression is a complicated one. One way to understand it better is to identify causes and effects. Work with a group of two or three classmates. Reread "The Great Depression." Identify each sentence that describes one of the hardships people faced. In your notebook, make a list of these hardships, or effects, of the Great Depression. Then go through this reading and earlier readings in this unit and see if you can find a cause for each of the effects.

When you have finished your lists of causes and effects, construct a graphic organizer that displays them. You may also want to illustrate your graphic organizer. Explain your group's graphic organizer to the rest of the class.

LEARNING STRATEGY

Reminder: Using a **graphic organizer** is a strategy that can help you organize complicated information so that it is easier to understand and remember.

Franklin D. Roosevelt

Identifying What You Know and Predicting

In this unit, you have studied the first thirty-one years of the twentieth century in the United States. Without looking back in this unit, make a list in your notebook of what you can remember about the important events and people of the beginning of the twentieth century. Share your list with a classmate. Did you forget anything important? Add it to your list.

Working with the same classmate, use the information that you remember to make predictions about what might have happened in the United States during the years 1932 to 1940. Write your predictions on a separate page in your notebook. When you finish this unit, you will look back at your predictions and see if you were right!

LEARNING STRATEGY

Reminder: Two strategies, **use what you know** and **predicting,** often work together. If you remember and understand what has already happened in history, this knowledge can give you good clues for predicting what might happen next.

Franklin Delano Roosevelt

A new president, Franklin Delano Roosevelt, was elected in 1932. (He was a distant relative of Theodore Roosevelt.) He won four presidential elections and would be president for the next twelve years—the longest time of any U.S. president.

There were two main challenges in Roosevelt's presidency. First, he had to get the United States out of the Depression. Second, he was president during a second world war. In both periods, he led the country with new ideas and made people believe that times would be better. When he first ran for president, his campaign theme song was "Happy Days Are Here Again."

THE NEW DEAL: RELIEF, RECOVERY, AND REFORM

When Roosevelt took office, he began right away to help people who were out of work, who had lost all of their money, or who had no place to live. Unlike President Hoover, Roosevelt decided that the best way to help Americans was to have the government provide money to get new ideas started. Roosevelt's programs were known as the New Deal.

Men plant trees for a CCC (Civilian Conservation Corps) project in Minnesota.

The programs that Roosevelt set up with Congress were called the Alphabet Soup Agencies and Acts because people referred to them by their initials. For farmers, the AAA (Agricultural Adjustment Act) tried to raise the price of crops; the REA (Rural Electrification Administration) brought electricity to rural areas; and the FSA (Farm Security Administration) provided loans so that farmers could keep their farms.

For labor, the NLRA (National Labor Relations Act) allowed workers to bargain about wages and working conditions; the FLSA (Fair Labor Standards Act) set a minimum wage of 25 cents an hour, set a maximum work week of 44 hours, and made it illegal to hire children under age sixteen.

To give general relief to people, the FERA (Federal Emergency Relief Administration) provided federal money to feed the poor and pay for local projects like building roads; the CCC (Civilian Conservation Corps) put unemployed young men to work on conservation projects; the FHA (Federal Housing Act) provided low-interest loans for house building and repair; and the WPA (Works Progress Administration) gave jobs to millions of workers to build roads, bridges, and public buildings. The WPA also hired artists, writers, and actors for public art projects. The National Youth Administration (NYA) provided part-time work to 16- to 25-year olds and allowed them to finish their education. The NHA (National Housing Act) gave money for low-income housing.

To help protect people against another economic depression, Roosevelt established the FDIC (Federal Deposit Insurance Corporation), which still exists today. It insures people's money when they deposit it in a bank. The SEC (Securities Exchange Act) was set up to regulate

A WPA (Works Progress Administration) crew rebuilds the Morris Canal, New Jersey.

the stock market, and the SSA (Social Security Act) of 1935 provided monthly payments to people over age sixty-five. All of these programs are still in effect today.

The effect of all these new federal government programs was to provide work for the unemployed, help for people who were suffering, and insurance against future economic problems. The United States began to recover, and people became optimistic about their future once again.

But this was just the beginning of Roosevelt's presidency. In the next unit, you will learn how he became a world leader in the international crisis of World War II.

UNDERSTANDING WHAT YOU READ Making a Graphic Organizer

How does the learning strategy making a **graphic organizer** help you understand new information? Write your answer in your notebook.

LEARNING STRATEGY

Work with one or more classmates. Create a graphic organizer that will help you remember the Alphabet Soup Agencies and Acts. Your graphic organizer should include the name of each agency and act and its initials, what it did, and which people it helped. If you need additional information, check your school library or the Internet.

When you are satisfied with your graphic organizer, show it and explain it to the rest of the class.

LISTENING AND TAKING NOTES

Copy the T-list below in your notebook. Then listen to information about the life of Eleanor Roosevelt, a woman remembered as a fighter for social justice. As you listen, take notes on the information using the T-list. The main ideas are written on the left. Write the details and examples on the right. After you listen, compare your notes with two or three classmates. Did you forget anything? If so, add it to your notes. Finally, use your notes to write in your notebook a summary of Eleanor Roosevelt's life.

LEARNING STRATEGY

Reminder: While you listen, focus on the information you need to fill in the details and examples. This learning strategy is called **selective attention**. It helps you find specific information while listening or reading. Write down the information using key words and abbreviations only, not complete sentences. This learning strategy is called **taking notes**. It helps you remember information later and can be a good study guide. Together, these two strategies can help you become a better student!

Eleanor Roosevelt

MAIN IDEAS	DETAILS AND EXAMPLES
A. Eleanor Roosevelt's early life	_____ _____ _____
B. Her active political life in New York and Washington, DC	_____ _____ _____ _____
C. Eleanor Roosevelt stands up for human rights	_____ _____ _____ _____
D. Why Eleanor Roosevelt is important	_____ _____ _____ _____

Important People of the Early Twentieth Century

Many men and women made important contributions to life in the United States between 1900 and 1940. These people included artists, aviators, business people, explorers, industrialists, inventors, movie stars, musicians, novelists, philanthropists (rich people who give money for museums, universities, for example), poets, and social reformers.

Your teacher will help you select an important person from the first part of the twentieth century to research and write a report about.

LEARNING STRATEGY

Reminder: When you look for information on a topic, you are **using resources**. You can find these resources in your school or public library and on the Internet. Use this learning strategy when you need more information than what is in your textbook.

RESEARCHING Finding the Information You Need

1. Look for information about the important person you have chosen. You may want to use biographies, an encyclopedia, and the Internet.

2. As you read, take notes on the important information about the person. Write your notes on index cards. Use a new card for each source. Use your own words except when noting quotations that you think are important. You need to find the following information:

   Complete name

   Dates of birth and death

   Early years and education

   Occupation

   Accomplishments

   Major contributions (why this person is important in U.S. history)

3. Look over your note cards. Do you need any more information?

1. Use your note cards to make an outline of your report. Complete the outline form below in your notebook. Add more items, if necessary.

> [TITLE OF REPORT]
>
> **I.** Introduction
>
> Tell what your report will be about by giving the name of the person and why he or she is important.
>
> **II.** Early Life
>
> A. Date of birth and family background
> B. Education
> C. Marriage, children
>
> **III.** Accomplishments
>
> A. What was outstanding about this person?
> B. Did this person make a difference in the lives of others?
> C. Are this person's contributions still in use today?
>
> **IV.** Conclusion
>
> Give a brief summary of the important facts in your report. Then summarize why your person is important in U.S. history.

2. When you complete your outline, you are ready to begin writing the first draft of your report. If possible, use a computer. This makes it easier to make revisions later.

1. Read through your report. Does it have all the important information about your person? Add anything that is missing.

2. Read through your report again. Have you repeated any information? Is there information that is not important to your biography? If so, take it out.

3. Now read your report aloud to a classmate. Is there something interesting you forgot to say? Ask for feedback. Take notes!

4. Now listen to your classmate's report. Give feedback that is helpful. If you are curious about something in your classmate's report, ask questions.

LEARNING STRATEGY

Discussing your report with others can help you make improvements. When you work with someone else, what learning strategy are you using? Write it in your notebook.

Checking Spelling, Punctuation, and Grammar

1. Carefully check the spelling in your report. If you are using a computer, use the spell-check feature. Then reread carefully—the spell-check feature will not correct all errors! For instance, if you wrote *red* when you really meant *read* (past tense), the spelling checker will not correct it. Correct all spelling mistakes. Use a dictionary, if necessary.

2. Now check punctuation and capitalization. Does every sentence start with a capital letter? Do all names of places and people start with capital letters? Do all sentences end with a period, a question mark, or an exclamation mark? Are there commas between clauses in long sentences? Did you use quotation marks before and after quotes? Did you indent each paragraph? Correct any errors.

3. Now check the grammar. Remember to check the following:
   - Present tense, third-person singular ends in -s (she say<u>s</u>)
   - Adjectives come before nouns (a <u>poor</u> family)
   - Most verbs in a biography will be in the <u>past</u> tense (She <u>began</u> writing poetry when she <u>was</u> fifteen years old.)

   Check with your teacher if you are not sure about grammar.

4. Read your report one last time. Are you satisfied? Is it the best work you can do? If so, turn it in to your teacher.

PRESENTING AN ORAL REPORT

Sit in a small group with three other classmates. Read your reports to each other. Be ready to answer questions after reading your report. In your notebook, write three important facts that you learned from listening to each classmate's report.

Gangster Al Capone controlled the Chicago underworld.

Journalist and activist Ida B. Wells

Writer Langston Hughes, a major figure of the Harlem Renaissance

Eight Presidents: 1900–1940

Eight presidents served from 1900 until 1940. They made many decisions about what was important for the United States. You have already read about several of the presidents during this period. The time line below shows all of the presidents and some of the laws that were passed and the events that occurred during their terms in office.

	PRESIDENT	EVENTS
–1900	William F. McKinley	
	Theodore Roosevelt	1901 – McKinley assassinated; Theodore Roosevelt becomes president
		1902 – Helps settle coal strike
		1903 – National Reclamation Act passed to help preserve wilderness
		Wright Brothers fly the first airplane
		Platt Amendment allows naval base at Guantánamo Bay, Cuba
		U.S. recognizes Panama as independent from Colombia
		1904 – U.S. granted ownership of Canal Zone by Panama; digging of Panama Canal begins
–1905		1905 – International Workers of the World (IWW) union organized
		U.S. Forest Service established
		1906 – Pure Food and Drug Act passed
		1907 – President sends U.S. ships around the world to show U.S. power
	William Howard Taft	
–1910		1910 – NAACP founded by W.E.B. DuBois
		1911 – Triangle Shirtwaist factory fire
		Supreme Court orders Standard Oil Company monopoly to be split into different companies
		1912 – U.S. Marines occupy Nicaragua (1912–1933), Veracruz, Mexico, and Haiti and Dominican Republic to protect U.S. interests
	Woodrow Wilson	1913 – 16th Amendment (income tax)
		17th Amendment (direct election of senators)
		Huge march for women's suffrage in New York City
–1915		
		1916 – National Park Service created
		1917 – Eight-hour day for railroad workers
		U.S. involved in World War I (1917–1918)
		Lenin seizes power in Russia
		1919 – 18th Amendment (Prohibition)
		Treaty of Versailles brings peace; League of Nations established
		Racial violence in Chicago
–1920		1920 – 19th Amendment (women's suffrage)
		Restrictive immigration laws passed (1920–1929)
		Marcus Garvey and the "Back to Africa" movement
	Warren G. Harding	1921 – Teapot Dome Scandal over oil rights (1921–1923)
		Harlem Renaissance (1921–1929)
	Calvin Coolidge	1923 – Harding dies; Calvin Coolidge becomes president
–1925		
		1927 – First sound movie, *The Jazz Singer*
		Charles Lindbergh flies solo across the Atlantic Ocean
	Herbert Hoover	1929 – Stock market crashes
		The Great Depression (1929–1939)

1930		
	Franklin Delano Roosevelt	1933 – The New Deal (1933–1938) First female Cabinet member, Frances Perkins, Secretary of Labor Repeal of 18th Amendment
1935		
		1937 – Constitutional challenges to the New Deal (1937–1938)
		1939 – New York World's Fair
1940		1940 – Franklin Delano Roosevelt re-elected president for third term

UNDERSTANDING WHAT YOU READ **Classifying Events**

The time line on pages 60–61 shows some of the major events that happened during the terms of the U.S. presidents in the first forty years of the twentieth century. Sometimes these changes affected almost everybody. Sometimes they affected only certain groups.

Work with two or three classmates. Look at each event on the time line. Decide who was affected most by this event. Almost everyone? Workers? Women? Minorities? A particular business or industry? Other countries? Was the effect good or bad for those it affected? (Hint: You will have to do research in the school library or on the Internet to find out more about some of these events.)

LEARNING STRATEGY

When you sort information into categories, you are using a learning strategy named **classification**. When you classify, you put things that have similarities together in a group. This can help you remember important information.

As your group finds out more about each event, decide on a good category for that event. Some events may fit into more than one category. On a separate sheet of paper, make a chart that shows your group's categories and the events for each.

Now write what you predict will happen next for each category of event on the chart in your notebook. Then share your chart and your predictions with the class.

LEARNING STRATEGY

Reminder: Use what you already know to predict what might happen next. Using the learning strategy **predicting** gets you ready to learn more about a particular topic.

The United States Becomes a World Leader: 1940–1960

Tell what you think

Events in the world would affect the United States over the twenty years from 1940 to 1960 as it expanded its role in world affairs.

- What happens during a depression?
- What did President Roosevelt do to solve the problems caused by the Depression in the United States?
- How might war solve the problems caused by a depression?

Write your ideas in your notebook.

In this unit you will

- learn about the involvement of the United States in World War II
- learn about Nazism, communism, and fascism
- research the lives of important men and women of this period
- learn how the United States became a world power
- find out more about U.S. civil rights
- use maps, charts, photographs, and historical documents to find out about another time in history
- sharpen your listening, speaking, and note-taking skills, and write your own reports

TIME LINE   1940

1941
Pearl Harbor attacked

1945

1945
Atomic bombs
dropped on Japan

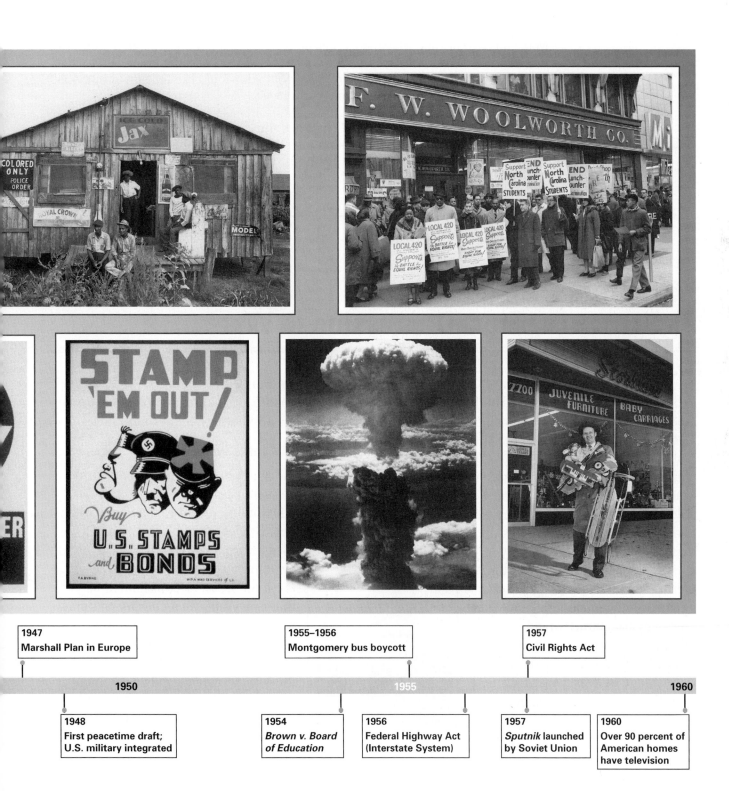

1947
Marshall Plan in Europe

1955–1956
Montgomery bus boycott

1957
Civil Rights Act

1950

1955

1960

1948
First peacetime draft;
U.S. military integrated

1954
*Brown v. Board
of Education*

1956
Federal Highway Act
(Interstate System)

1957
Sputnik launched
by Soviet Union

1960
Over 90 percent of
American homes
have television

LEARNING STRATEGY

Reminder: You can understand new information better when you think back about related information that you have already studied. The name of this learning strategy is **use what you know**.

Aftermath refers to events that happen as a result of one important event. In Unit 2 you read about some of the events that were part of the aftermath of World War I. How many of these events can you remember?

Work with two or three classmates. Talk about what happened in different countries in Europe after World War I. Talk about both the winners and the losers. After you talk about what you already know, discuss what you would like to learn about what happened in Europe in the 1930s and early 1940s.

In your notebook, make a *K-W-L-H* chart like the model below. Write sentences to complete the *K* (What We Already *K*now) column. Write questions to complete the *W* (What We *W*ant to Find Out) column. You will complete the *L* and *H* columns later.

K	W	L	H

From Depression to War

Germany and the other countries that lost in World War I, such as Austria-Hungary and Bulgaria, were very poor after the war ended in 1918. The nations that won the war (the Allies) wanted Germany to pay for all of the damage caused by the war. Germany's casualties amounted to over 60 percent of their 11 million soldiers who fought. Their factories and farms had been terribly damaged, and people were starving. The Allies did not want Germany to be able to fight a war again, so they made it difficult for Germany to rebuild. Many Germans were very angry at the Allies for blaming them for all of the damage of World War I. Little by little, the Germans began to build up their country again.

In contrast, the Allies had greater resources. There had been no battles fought on U.S. soil, and U.S. factories and farms had been making supplies for the rest of the Allies and helping them to rebuild.

EUROPEAN LEADERS WITH DIFFERENT IDEAS

After the Russian Revolution and World War I, there were people in Europe who became interested in the ideas of the new Soviet leader, V. I. Lenin. His ideas were formed into a political system called *communism*. One of the main ideas of communism is that everything in a country (natural resources, factories, farms, and businesses) is owned by the state (the government) instead of by individual owners. In Russia, many people who had owned factories, shops, or farms had them taken away by the leaders of the Revolution.

Soviet leader V. I. Lenin

There were some groups of people in Italy, Spain, and Germany who thought that they might have better lives under a communist government. Other people and governments in non-communist countries began to fear the ideas of communism.

THE RISE OF FASCISM

Another new idea about government, called *fascism*, began in Italy in 1922 and spread to other European nations. The most important belief in fascism is that a person be totally loyal to the state. Fascism was started in Italy by Benito Mussolini, who had come to power after World War I. He believed that a good government was one that strictly controlled the nation and individual lives. He ruled as a dictator—a leader with absolute power. Mussolini's ideas of fascism spread to Spain and Germany. In Spain, General Francisco Franco led a revolt against the Spanish Republic, starting the Spanish Civil War. This war lasted from 1936 until Franco took power in 1939 as a fascist dictator. The German leader, Adolf Hitler, helped Franco win his war.

HITLER RISES TO POWER IN GERMANY

Germany worked hard to recover after World War I. It went through a severe depression in the 1920s, but then life began to get better. In 1933, Adolf Hitler and his group called the Nazi Party became popular. Many members of his party won elections, and Hitler was appointed chancellor, or leader, of the Republic of Germany. People voted for him because he talked about getting the other European countries to respect Germany again. People were tired of war and of being poor and hungry, and they did not like being hated by the rest of the European countries. They believed that Hitler could make their lives better.

In 1933, members of the Nazi Party took control of Germany and made Hitler a dictator. He threatened people who did not agree with him, and he ignored the World War I

Benito Mussolini

Francisco Franco

Adolf Hitler

"From each according to his ability; to each according to his need."
—Communist motto

treaty. He began to manufacture weapons and rebuild an army. He blamed Jews (and others who he did not think were "pure" Germans) for all of Germany's problems. He began to identify and arrest these people. He also made alliances with other dictatorships, such as the one in Italy. The democratic countries in Europe, mainly France and Britain, formed alliances and used the policy of appeasement in a desperate effort to avoid war.

Japan Takes Chinese Territory

Japan was also suffering from a depression in the 1930s. Ruled by a powerful emperor, it was a small country with a growing population. It wanted to have more land to increase its resources. In 1931–1932, Japan saw an opportunity to move into and take over a large area of northeastern China called Manchuria. China was too weak to fight and the western nations did not react, so Japan kept Manchuria.

Japanese Emperor Hirohito

UNDERSTANDING WHAT YOU READ Summarizing

LEARNING STRATEGY

Reminder: After reading, write down the most important ideas in your own words. This strategy is called **summarizing**.

In your notebook, write one or two sentences that express the main ideas in each section of "From Depression to War." Check your summary with a classmate. Did you answer these questions in your summary?

1. What were the problems in Germany after World War I?

2. What is the main idea of communism?

3. What is the main idea of fascism?

4. Who was Mussolini? What did he do?

5. Who was Franco? What did he do?

6. Who was Hitler? What did he do?

7. What happened in Asia in the early 1930s?

Jesse Owens

HISTORY MYSTERY

In 1936, the Olympic Games were held in Berlin, Germany. American runner Jesse Owens won four gold medals. What made Hitler unhappy about Jesse Owens winning these medals?

Use the Glossary to find the meanings of the words below. Then write the words and their meanings in your notebook, using your own words. Do not copy the Glossary definition.

conquer	alliance	overthrow
invade	ally (pl. allies)	surrender

Conflicts Rapidly Expand into War

The First World War (1914–1918) was supposed to have been "the war to end all wars." But very soon the world was involved in an even bigger war. In the years 1935–1939, Germany and Italy took over land outside their borders. Italy conquered Ethiopia (in Africa), and Germany invaded parts of France and Austria. Hitler and Mussolini supported the Spanish Civil War. At that time, President Roosevelt signed a law saying the United States would remain neutral.

Alliances were forming among the nations that wanted to gain more land. Germany and Italy formed an alliance called the Axis powers. Germany had taken over Austria and Czechoslovakia. Italy took over Albania. Japan invaded China. Hitler signed an agreement with Stalin (the Soviet leader since 1929) not to attack the Soviet Union. Japan also had an agreement with Russia not to attack its eastern border. But Japan continued to take land in other areas of East Asia. The United States became concerned about protecting its trade with countries in East Asia, but still it remained neutral.

On September 1, 1939, Hitler's army invaded Poland without warning. Britain and France declared war on Germany. World War II had begun.

Europe in Flames

In 1940, the German army conducted a *blitzkrieg*, which means a "lightning war," or a war that moves very rapidly. On April 9, 1940, it invaded and conquered Denmark in just one day. It then moved on to conquer Norway in

German tanks roll into Poland.

less than three weeks, turned south, and by May 10 had conquered Belgium and the Netherlands. By May 21, the German army had arrived at the English Channel. On June 10, 1940, Italy entered the war as an ally of Germany. France was defeated by German forces by June 14; on June 22, the French delegates surrendered to Hitler. This surrender took place in the same railroad car at Compiègne, France, where German delegates had been forced to sign the Treaty of Versailles after they had been defeated in World War I in 1918.

The German army marches into Paris.

The blitzkrieg had lasted little more than two months, and at its end Germany had control of most of western Europe. Italy was fighting along with Germany, and by September 1940 Japan had also joined the Axis powers.

In spite of its non-aggression agreement with the Soviet Union, Germany invaded it in 1941. The Soviet Union then joined the Allies (Britain and France) to fight the Axis powers.

THE BATTLE OF BRITAIN

After the surrender of France, Britain stood alone, as the United States had not yet entered the war and Russia was under attack. Instead of physically invading Britain, Germany sent airplanes and rockets to bomb important British cities and supply ships. The bombs fell almost every day from July through October 1940.

Although Germany's air force attacked Britain with almost non-stop bombing for over four months, Britain did not fall. The British prime minister, Winston Churchill, told the British people and Germany, "We shall not flag [lose interest] or fail. We shall go on to the end, we shall fight in France, we shall fight on the seas and oceans . . . we shall fight in the fields and in the streets, we shall fight in the hills; we shall never surrender."

Winston Churchill

Belgian refugees on the road to France

The ruins of a London neighborhood after bombing by the Germans

British civilians take shelter from air raids in an underground railroad station.

UNDERSTANDING WHAT YOU READ Using Maps

Study the map of Europe on page 69. In your notebook, list the Axis powers and the Allies. For each country that the German army conquered during the blitzkrieg, write that date by the name of the country. What Axis power is not on this map?

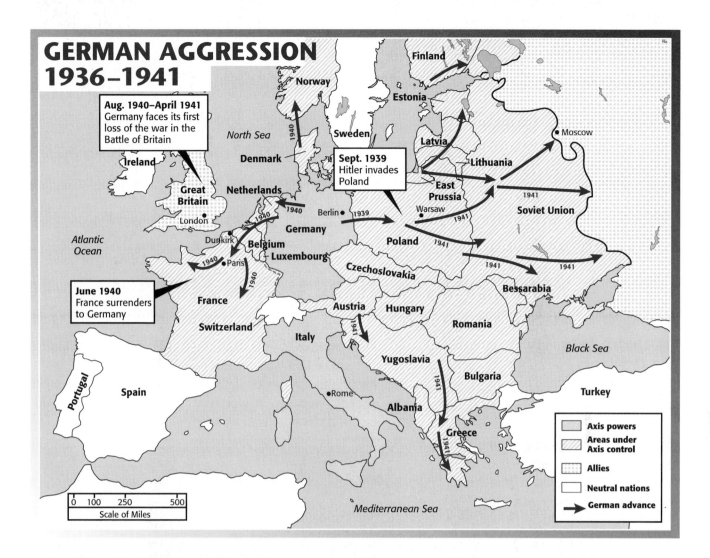

GERMAN AGGRESSION 1936–1941

Aug. 1940–April 1941
Germany faces its first loss of the war in the Battle of Britain

Sept. 1939
Hitler invades Poland

June 1940
France surrenders to Germany

Finland
Norway
Estonia
Sweden
Latvia
Moscow
Lithuania
North Sea
Denmark
Ireland
Great Britain
London
Netherlands
East Prussia
Berlin
Warsaw
Soviet Union
Atlantic Ocean
Germany
Poland
Dunkirk
Belgium
Luxembourg
Paris
Czechoslovakia
Bessarabia
France
Austria
Hungary
Switzerland
Italy
Romania
Black Sea
Yugoslavia
Bulgaria
Spain
Portugal
Rome
Turkey
Albania
Greece
Mediterranean Sea

0 100 250 500
Scale of Miles

Axis powers
Areas under Axis control
Allies
Neutral nations
German advance

UNDERSTANDING WHAT YOU READ Focusing on Your Learning

1. Now meet with the same group of classmates you worked with to begin your *K-W-L-H* chart in the Before You Read activity on page 64. What new information have you learned about Europe after World War I? What happened in different European countries?

2. Read what you wrote in the *K* (What We Already *K*now) column for the activity. Do you need to correct any facts that you listed? If so, do it now.

3. Read what you wrote in the *W* (What We *W*ant to Find Out) column. Were your questions answered? Check off the questions that were answered. Now look for answers to the questions that still need to be answered. Use an encyclopedia or the Internet.

4. Write sentences in the *L* (What We *L*earned) column to tell what you learned about events in Europe after World War I.

5. Talk with your classmates about how you learned the new information. Write the learning strategies that you used in the *H* (*H*ow We Learned) column. Share your group's *K-W-L-H* chart with the rest of the class.

Why do you think the United States wanted to stay out of the war in Europe? Why do you think the United States finally did enter the war?

Work with a classmate to discuss these questions. Write your answers in your notebook. Refer to your answers after you have read the next section.

When you use what you have already learned to think about what might happen next, what learning strategies are you using?

LEARNING STRATEGY

World War II and the United States

THE UNITED STATES WANTS TO STAY OUT OF WAR

In the 1930s, an opinion poll of Americans said that most did not want to get involved in a war. A peace movement grew among college students and, in the summer of 1936, half a million students across the country attended anti-war events. In October 1940, President Roosevelt said: "I have said this before, but I shall say it again and again and again: 'Your boys are not going to be sent into any foreign wars.'" In November, he said: "Your president says this country is not going to war."

Franklin Delano Roosevelt was running for president for a third term in 1940. No other president had served more than two terms. But in this uncertain time, people wanted to keep a president they knew, so they re-elected President Roosevelt for another four years.

The United States sent supplies and equipment to help Britain fight Germany. The arrangement to help Britain was called Lend-Lease. This meant that the United States was "lending" the equipment to Britain, although it did not really expect to have the equipment returned. President

Roosevelt explained that it was necessary to support Britain in this way in order to defend the Four Freedoms for which democracies fought: freedom of speech, freedom of worship, freedom from want, and freedom from fear.

The artist Norman Rockwell painted four paintings representing the four freedoms: *Speech, Worship, Want,* and *Fear.* Which freedom does this painting represent? How do you know?

The bombing of Pearl Harbor, Hawaii, by the Japanese, December 7, 1941

While the United States was trying to stay out of the war, Germany, Italy, and Japan continued to extend their power. Germany invaded the Soviet Union, even though the two countries had an agreement not to attack each other. Italy conquered Greece and British Somaliland (today Somalia) in Africa. Japan conquered French Indochina (today Vietnam).

THE UNITED STATES ENTERS THE WAR

In the end, the United States could not stay out of the war. Japan (an Axis power) bombed Pearl Harbor, Hawaii, in a surprise attack on December 7, 1941. In that bombing, 2,335 American soldiers and sailors were killed, 1,178 were wounded, and 200 airplanes and 14 Navy ships were destroyed or damaged. Calling December 7 "a date which will live in infamy," President Roosevelt asked Congress to declare war on Japan. On December 11, the United States also declared war on Germany and Italy.

President Franklin D. Roosevelt requests a declaration of war from Congress, December 8, 1941.

Now the United States was completely involved in World War II. The next four years became some of the most important of the twentieth century. The United States's strength was added to the fight against Germany, Japan, and Italy. This war would change the United States and the world.

Winning the War

The United States organized for victory in many ways. Study the images on these two pages to find out some of the things that people did to help win the war.

Workers build tanks in a U.S. factory. In 1942 alone, U.S. manufacturers produced 60,000 planes, 20,000 anti-aircraft guns, 45,000 tanks, and 8 million tons of supplies.

Thousands of men and women signed up to fight: 350,000 women, 25,000 Native Americans, 350,000 Mexican Americans, 1 million African Americans, and 33,000 Japanese Americans.

Community members gather in support of the war effort by growing their own food in "victory gardens."

Across the nation, more than 450,000 tons of recycled rubber were collected for use on military vehicles.

Thousands more, especially women and African Americans, started working in factories to make goods for war. They had not been allowed to work in these jobs before the war. By 1945, 6 million women—equal to over one-third of all workers—were working in factories.

Many Japanese Americans—adults as well as children—were placed in internment camps by the U.S. government. As many as 112,000 people lost their land, homes, or businesses.

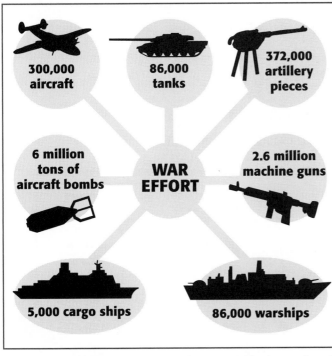

By 1945, the United States had produced more material for the war than all Axis countries combined.

Posters from the United States and Britain encouraged people to help at home.

UNDERSTANDING WHAT YOU READ | Using Images

Work with a classmate. Study the images, and make a list in your notebook of the different experiences that people went through during the war. Share and compare your list with another pair of students.

LEARNING STRATEGY

Reminder: The strategy **using imagery** can help you understand what life was like in a particular period of history. Study the images carefully, and talk about the story they tell.

The United States Joins the Allies

The war was not going well for the Allies when the United States entered the fight in 1941. Once the United States joined in, however, it put all its personal and governmental power into winning. New inventions such as rockets, along with better airplanes and submarines, improved tanks and more powerful weapons, and improved radar and sonar, finally began to give the Allies an advantage.

The war began to shift when the Allies won some victories. For example, the Soviet (Russian) army saved the city of Stalingrad from German attack and began to drive the Germans out of Russia. In the war against Japan in the Pacific, the United States won important battles at Midway and Guadalcanal, though at great cost in numbers of U.S. soldiers' lives lost.

UNDERSTANDING WHAT YOU READ | **Using Maps**

Look at the map below and the map on page 149. Then answer the questions about the end of World War II that are below and on page 149. Write your answers in your notebook.

1. In what state is Pearl Harbor?
2. What battles did the United States lose against Japan? What battles did the United States win against Japan?
3. How would you describe the strategy used by the Allies to defeat Japan?
4. Where and when were the battles of Midway and Guadalcanal fought?

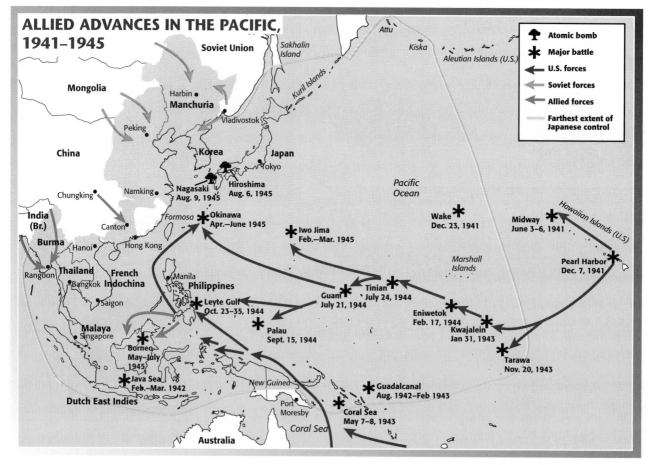

ALLIED ADVANCES IN THE PACIFIC, 1941–1945

Legend:
- Atomic bomb
- Major battle
- U.S. forces
- Soviet forces
- Allied forces
- Farthest extent of Japanese control

The Code Talkers

LISTENING AND TAKING NOTES

You will listen to a true story about some important heroes of World War II. Their story was a secret for many years after the war, but finally the story was told. In 2000, Congress passed a special bill to honor these heroes. In July 2001, five of the surviving twenty-nine original Code Talkers were presented with congressional gold medals in a ceremony at the Capitol in Washington, DC.

Copy the T-list below in your notebook. As you listen to the story of the Code Talkers, take notes on the information using the T-list. The main ideas are written on the left. Write the details and examples on the right. After you listen, compare your notes with two or three classmates. Did you forget anything? If so, add it to your notes. Finally, use your notes to write in your own words what you learned about the Code Talkers. Use complete sentences and paragraphs.

Navajo Code Talkers

Reminder: Use **selective attention** to decide what information to write down. Use **taking notes** to write down the key ideas.

LEARNING STRATEGY

MAIN IDEAS	DETAILS AND EXAMPLES
A. Who the Code Talkers were	1. _____ 2. _____
B. Why a code was needed	1. _____ 2. _____ 3. _____
C. How the code was developed and used	1. _____ 2. _____ 3. _____ 4. _____
D. Why the code Talkers were important	1. _____ 2. _____ 3. _____

BEFORE YOU READ | Using Headings

Look at the three headings in the next reading. Then read the questions below. In which portion do you think you will find the answer to each question? Write the headings in your notebook. Then scan the sections to find the answers to the questions. Write the answers in your notebook under the correct heading.

LEARNING STRATEGY

What learning strategy are you using when you try to find specific information in a reading?

1. What happened in Berlin, Germany, when the war was over?

2. How was Japan defeated by the United States?

3. What was the date of the end of the war against Germany?

4. What two Japanese cities were destroyed by atomic bombs?

5. What was the name of the general who led the invasion of Europe?

The Axis Powers Are Defeated

GERMANY IS DEFEATED

On a cloudy day in June 1944, the Allied troops, led by the U.S. General Dwight David Eisenhower, began the invasion of Europe at Normandy, France. This final Allied drive to defeat Germany was known as the D-Day invasion. It was a very difficult attack, and many soldiers died because the Germans had weapons built into the beaches. For the next year, the Allies fought across Europe toward Berlin, Germany's capital. On May 6, 1945, Hitler committed suicide in Berlin. On May 8, Germany surrendered to the Allies. This day would be known as V-E Day (Victory in Europe).

JAPAN SURRENDERS

Japan continued to fight in the Pacific. To win the war against Japan, the Allied forces had to attack one island after another in the Pacific. This was extremely difficult, because the Japanese military forces had many weapons

U.S. troops advance into Germany

already on the islands. The Allies were losing many men in these battles, and they believed that thousands more would die.

The United States, however, had a weapon that it had been developing secretly since 1942. This was the atomic bomb (the A-bomb). The United States had just two of these bombs, and it dropped them on two Japanese cities, Hiroshima (August 6) and Nagasaki (August 8). Almost 200,000 people were killed or missing, and a third to a half of each city was destroyed. Japan surrendered.

The world was glad the war was over, but also horrified by the effects of the atomic bomb. Not only did the A-bombs kill many people and destroy many buildings, their fallout also spread radioactivity over a large area. The bombs' radioactivity burned the skin of survivors and made them ill with diseases such as cancer. Radioactivity also contaminated large areas of land and water, making it difficult for people to live in those areas.

Hiroshima after the atomic bomb

THE EFFECTS OF WORLD WAR II

The loss of human life in World War II was immense—more than 44 million military and civilian people from the Allied nations died. In the Axis countries, more than 11 million people died. Because the war was not fought in the United States itself, the United States had few civilian casualties, but more than 300,000 military people died.

Hitler's program to develop a master race was devastating to Jews, Gypsies, political enemies, and others Hitler hated. It resulted in the deaths of 12 million people, 6 million of them Jews. Most of those deaths occurred in concentration camps. These were large, prison-like places where Hitler sent people who he wanted to kill. The Nazis rounded up men, women, and children and transported them by train to the concentration camps. The conditions in these camps were inhumane, and many people suffered torture and starvation before being killed. This mass killing of people, or genocide, became known as the Holocaust.

Following the end of the war in 1945, the Allies began the recovery by establishing the United Nations, with a goal of world peace. Fifty-one nations agreed to work together. But throughout the world, the recovery would be hard because many challenges stood in the way of peace.

For a time at the end of the war, the Allies divided Germany and its capital, Berlin, into four parts, or sectors. The sectors were controlled by Britain, France, the United States, and the Soviet Union. By 1948, the Allies were ready to allow the Germans to reunite into a single country. But Berlin was located inside the Soviet sector, and the Soviets decided that they would keep the other nations out.

The other Allies began what was called the Berlin Airlift. This was an amazing project that flew supplies into West Berlin twenty-four hours a day to keep the people from starving. Finally, the Soviet Union allowed the other Allies into West Berlin. But they kept the eastern sector of Germany closed off, and the country remained divided into West Germany and East Germany for the next forty years.

In 1947, the United States also developed the Marshall Plan to help European countries that had been damaged by the war. It was named after Secretary of State George C. Marshall, who had first suggested the plan. The plan offered basic aid to all European countries to help them rebuild after the war. It worked well because it gave people food and work to begin rebuilding. The Soviet Union and the countries it controlled did not participate in the recovery plan.

The United States was now a leader in the world. Even though some people in the United States wanted to stay out of international affairs, the nation would never be able to do so again.

U.S. cargo planes bring food to the German people, Berlin, 1948.

When you study historical events, it is important to try to understand why each event happened. This is called *cause* (the reason) and *effect* (what happened). Very often, the effect of one event or situation becomes the cause of another event. Some causes may have more than one effect, and some effects may have more than one cause.

Work with a classmate. In your notebook, make a chart like the one below. Then complete the missing causes and effects.

> "Our policy is directed not against country or doctrine, but against hunger, poverty, desperation, and chaos."
>
> —George C. Marshall, *Harvard Commencement, June 5, 1947*

CAUSES AND EFFECTS IN WORLD WAR II

CAUSE	EFFECT
Hitler invaded Poland.	
	In May 1940, Britain was without allies.
	The United States sent supplies and equipment to Britain.
Japan attacked Pearl Harbor.	
The United States needed to send secret messages in the war against Japan.	
	Six million Jews were killed in concentration camps.
The United States led the Normandy invasion (D-Day).	
	The United States dropped the A-bombs on Japan.
Radioactivity from the A-bombs spread over large areas.	
People in Berlin were starving after the war.	
	The United States started the Marshall Plan.
	The United States was recognized as a world leader.

Think about It!

How many different words can you find in this unit that refer to *Russia* or *Russians*? Why do you think that there were different words used at different times? What is this country, and what are its people called today? Why?

Write your ideas in your notebook.

Think and Make Predictions

After World War II, life in the United States boomed in different ways. As you read, look for four examples of booms in the post-war period.

Work with a group of classmates. Discuss how life in the United States might have changed after World War II. Remember, peace meant that all the soldiers came home. The United States no longer had to spend money on fighting a war. Predict what kinds of things might have boomed. Write your group's predictions in your notebook. Share them with the class.

Boom Times

Winning the war changed life in the United States. Factories, farms, and labor unions were larger, and the federal government was more powerful.

After 1945, the factories changed from production for war to making items for peacetime. The economy boomed. This meant that there were more jobs, more products, higher salaries, and higher prices. Many women who had been working in factories during the war left their jobs to stay home and raise families. The number of children born from 1946 to 1966 was the largest of any time in U.S. history. The population of the country grew by almost 40 million people, an increase of over 18 percent. This large increase in the birth rate was called the *baby boom*.

Congress passed the GI Bill of Rights in 1944. This bill was to help soldiers returning from the war adjust to life back home. The bill gave them money to set up farms or businesses, or to pay for education at a college or technical school. Many soldiers returning from the war used this money to start or finish college. The GI Bill was so successful that about 45,000 people used it from 1944 to 1951. The number of new college students in this time was almost

A Levittown housing development, Long Island, 1950s

double the pre-war numbers—creating a college boom.

People began to buy consumer goods such as washers and dryers, cars, and furniture. Home ownership increased, as many people could now afford to buy their own homes. During the housing boom in the 1950s, 13 million new homes were built. About 85 percent of those new homes were in the suburbs rather than the cities. People wanted to move to places outside the cities where they would have more space to raise their families. They used their cars to commute to work in the cities.

Checking Your Predictions

Work with the same group you worked with before reading about life in the United States after World War II. How many booms were you able to find? Check your predictions. How many were correct? Revise any incorrect predictions. Share them with the class.

The baby boom in the United States continued for twenty years. What effects do you think this sudden increase in children had on life in the United States?

Work with a group of two or three classmates. Discuss these questions and write your ideas in your notebook. Then share your group's ideas with the class.

1. What probably happened in 1952, when the baby boomers born in 1946 were six years old? And in 1959, when they became teenagers?

2. What probably happened when baby boomers started looking for jobs?

3. What probably happened when baby boomers decided to buy homes?

4. What is happening right now to the baby boomers?

Prejudice Follows the Soldiers Home

Groups of people such as Native Americans, African Americans, Japanese Americans, Hispanics, and women, whose rights had been limited before World War II, were very involved in the war effort. They had worked in factories during the war, fought in the war, or worked for the government to win the war. These people now sought the equal rights they had not had before or during the war.

There were some people who continued to be prejudiced. President Truman was very disturbed by the violence against African Americans in the South, including war veterans, who were pushing for their right to vote. He called for an end to *segregation* (separation of different groups, in this case blacks and whites). While his opinion on the issue of civil rights made him unpopular with some southerners, he believed that he was right. The president ordered the *integration*

(mixing of all groups) of the military and outlawed *discrimination* (favoring one group over another) in hiring any federal workers. The Supreme Court declared segregation on interstate buses unconstitutional and ruled against any rental or sale agreement that left out any group of people.

A poll tax was required of all people in the South who wanted to vote. The tax affected poor people, most of whom were African American.

Think about It

Prejudice means hating a group of people because of their race, their religion, or their ethnic or national origin. Work with a classmate to list examples in history when prejudice occurred. In your opinion, what could help reduce prejudice among groups of people? Write your personal ideas about prejudice in two or three paragraphs in your notebook.

BEFORE YOU READ | **Making Predictions**

Work with a group of two or three classmates. Discuss what the United States did in World War II and what changes in U.S. foreign policy might have happened as a result of actions and events in World War II.

When you think about what might happen next as a result of an event, what learning strategy are you using?

LEARNING STRATEGY

Write your group's ideas in your notebooks. Share them with the rest of the class.

A New Kind of War

President Roosevelt died just before the end of World War II (April 1945), and the vice president, Harry S Truman, became president. Americans were now confident that they could meet any challenge and that the new United Nations, formed at the end of World War II, would be able to establish and maintain a just and lasting peace.

But differences still existed in the world. The Soviet Union had been holding on to territory it occupied at the end of the war. The United States, Britain, France, and other allies believed that each country should be free to have its own government. The Soviet Union wanted to keep communist governments in all the territory it occupied after the war. Communist and non-communist countries began to build or rebuild their militaries and to form alliances with countries with similar governments.

The United States supported the non-communist nations. The Soviet Union, which had been one of the Allies in World War II, was now opposed to those nations.

POLICY OF CONTAINMENT

The Soviet Union developed the A-bomb in 1949. Now both the United States and the Soviet Union had the terrible power of the A-bomb. They did not directly attack each other with weapons. Instead, they fought each other through words or threats of war in what was called the *Cold War*.

The United States developed a policy to contain communism within the Soviet Union so that the Soviets could not force any other countries to take that form of government. The wars the United States fought over the next thirty years were based on this policy of containment.

U.S. Marines on a mountain road in Korea

One of these wars was fought in Korea. When North Korean communists invaded South Korea in 1950, the United Nations asked for assistance from member countries. President Truman ordered the U.S. military to lead the way. Although it is called the Korean War, it was never a war declared by Congress; instead it was called a "police action." It resulted in the deaths of more than 33,000 Americans and 100,000 wounded or missing; South Korea lost about 1 million people, and North Korea lost 1.5 million. The final cease-fire agreement in 1955 ended the killing but kept Korea divided into northern and southern sections. The north was communist and the south was democratic. This is still true today.

The Vietnam War was fought by the United States to try to prevent Ho Chi Minh, the communist leader in North Vietnam, from taking over South Vietnam. The United States also believed that if it did not contain communism in Vietnam, all of the other countries in Southeast Asia would become communist. You will learn more about the Vietnam War in the next unit when we talk about the 1960s.

UNDERSTANDING WHAT YOU READ **Checking Your Predictions**

Work with the same group you worked with before reading about the Cold War. Check your predictions. How many were correct? Revise any incorrect predictions. Share them with the class.

Reminder: **Predicting** is a learning strategy to help you better understand what you read. Everybody makes incorrect predictions, but predicting helps you think about what actually happened and why.

LEARNING STRATEGY

1. Think about what you have already learned in this unit. Without looking back in this book, quickly write down in your notebook everything you can remember about:

   - communism
   - the atomic bomb
   - General Eisenhower
   - the Cold War

2. Discuss what you have written with a classmate. If your classmate remembered items that you forgot, add these to your notes.

3. Share your combined notes with two other students. Add their notes.

LEARNING STRATEGY

When you think about what you already know about a topic before you read more information related to that topic, what learning strategy are you using?

Cold War Fears

FROM GENERAL TO PRESIDENT

In 1952, General Eisenhower, who had by then retired from the Army, ran for president. Richard Nixon was the vice presidential candidate. Eisenhower ("Ike") was a popular war hero, and Senator Nixon was a leader of the anti-communism movement of the late 1940s. Some voters in 1952 believed it was time for a change; some feared communism. Eisenhower and Nixon won 55 percent of the popular vote and took office in January 1953.

A political button with an Eisenhower campaign slogan

ANTI-COMMUNISM AFFECTS PEOPLE'S RIGHTS

There is no law in the United States against joining a political party or believing whatever you want, as long as you do not suggest overthrowing the government. In 1952, people in the United States were uneasy about the Soviet Union and its leader, Josef Stalin. Stalin had taken power from Lenin in 1925 and was aggressive in spreading communism.

In the United States, Senator Joseph McCarthy built on people's fear of communism. He began a campaign that accused many people in government, in unions, and in Hollywood of being communists. Although he often had no proof, many people supported him because they were afraid. Congress even passed laws that prevented some people from immigrating and kept others from working at certain types of jobs because McCarthy suggested that they might be communists. Finally, in 1954, the Senate censured Senator McCarthy for the way he accused people without proof, and he lost his power in Congress.

FEAR OF ATOMIC WAR

The fear of an attack by the Soviet Union was real for many people in the United States. They knew the damage an atomic bomb could cause from seeing the effects of the bombs in Japan. They knew that the Communist government in the Soviet Union had the bomb. Both the United States and the

A builder looks over plans for a backyard bomb shelter, 1951.

Soviet Union were building missiles that could send a nuclear bomb to the other country. The radioactive material from the bomb could kill or injure millions of people. This made people even more afraid of the Soviet Union.

Some of those who bought the new homes outside the cities were afraid that the Cold War might become "hot" and that the atomic bomb might be dropped near them. So some people built shelters in their backyards to protect their families in case of a bomb attack. There were also buildings in every city that could be used as shelters in case of an attack. Even today, we can see the shelter signs on some of these buildings.

Children practiced "duck and dive" in classrooms across the country.

UNDERSTANDING WHAT YOU READ Summarizing

Use the three headings in the reading about the Cold War to write down the main ideas in your own words.

LEARNING STRATEGY

What learning strategy are you using when you write or tell the most important ideas? Why is this a good learning strategy?

UNDERSTANDING WHAT YOU READ Using Images

In the 1950s, people were fearful of the atomic bomb and the effects of radioactivity. Look at the movie poster. Discuss with a classmate how such images might have made people even more afraid. Write your ideas in your notebook and share them with the class.

A poster of the 1954 movie *Godzilla*, a monster mutated by radiation fallout from atomic bombs

BEFORE YOU READ **Using Context**

Work with a classmate. Discuss each of the following vocabulary words. What do you think each word might mean? Write down your ideas in your notebook. Then, as you read, look at the context for each vocabulary word. Does the context help you understand the word better? If so, revise your definition.

LEARNING STRATEGY

Reminder: When you use context to help you understand new words, you are using the learning strategy **making inferences**.

interstate	unconstitutional	civil rights
segregation	doctrine	unmanned

Social and Technological Changes

EISENHOWER'S PROGRAMS

Sometimes when we look back at the past, we can see how things that happened influence our lives in the present. Some events and new laws that happened during the time of Eisenhower's presidency still affect us today.

Because people were moving out of the cities and were using their cars more and more, the highways were becoming more crowded and dangerous. President Eisenhower began a new program to use federal money to help the states build a road system across the country. This was the start of the four-lane, faster, safer interstate highway system.

In 1954, the Supreme Court of the United States made an important decision. The Court said that segregation in schools was unconstitutional because segregation prevented African Americans from practicing their right to an equal education with white Americans. The case was called *Brown v. Board of*

Interstate highways in California

Education. (One of the lawyers arguing for school desegregation was Thurgood Marshall, who would become a justice of the Supreme Court in 1967.) The Supreme Court justices in 1954 agreed that "in the field of public education the doctrine of 'separate but equal' has no place." Many white people in the South did not like this decision and continued to try to keep their schools segregated.

In addition, a protest against segregated buses began in Montgomery, Alabama, in 1955 when Rosa Parks refused to give up her seat on a bus to a white person. She was arrested. For the next thirteen months, African Americans protested by not riding the buses in Montgomery. The bus company finally agreed to allow African Americans to sit anywhere on the buses.

To desegregate the schools, President Eisenhower had to call in troops to protect African American high school students as they tried to enter Central High School in Little Rock, Arkansas, in 1957. Finally, a *Civil Rights Act* in 1957 began to bring more rights to African Americans.

CHANGES IN TECHNOLOGY

The United States was shocked when the Soviet Union became the first country to launch an unmanned satellite into space. The satellite was called *Sputnik,* and its success brought many changes in the United States. This event started the "space race" between the United States and the Soviet Union. The U.S. government realized that more scientists and engineers were needed to develop the technology that would win the space race. So the government gave more money for science education, and more students studied science and engineering.

The Problem We All Live With, a painting by Norman Rockwell, shows an African American girl being escorted to school by federal marshals in Kansas in the 1950s.

Throughout the 1950s, the electronics industry grew. There were computers, but they were so big they occupied whole rooms! People did not have computers in their homes yet, but they did have televisions. Now more and more people had televisions, but all the programs were in black and white.

In 1950, 5 million Americans owned a television set; by 1960, 90 percent of American homes had a television. The 1960 presidential election was won by John F. Kennedy based to a large extent on how he looked on television.

Russian postage stamps show Laika, the dog sent into space aboard *Sputnik.*

UNDERSTANDING WHAT YOU READ | Making Predictions

Work with a small group of classmates. Discuss the events described in the reading:

- interstate highway system
- Supreme Court: *Brown v. Board of Education*
- Civil Rights Act
- new technology

How do you think these events affected the United States after 1960? Make predictions and write them in your notebook.

Inventors and Scientists of the Mid-Twentieth Century

Inventors and scientists were very important to the way World War II was fought and to the way people would live after the war. The names and major accomplishments of some of these inventors and scientists are shown below.

Dr. J. Robert Oppenheimer (1904–1967), physicist, leader of the team that built the atomic bomb

Dr. Grace Murray Hopper (1906–1992), U.S. Navy officer, mathematician, developer of computer code COBOL

Dr. Albert Sabin (1906–1993), doctor, inventor of oral polio vaccine

Admiral Hyman Rickover (1900–1986), U.S. Navy officer, responsible for first nuclear-powered submarine

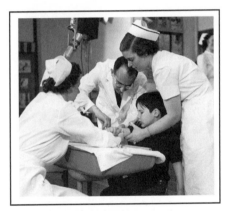

Dr. Jonas Salk (1914–1995), physician, inventor of Salk vaccine against polio

Dr. Charles Drew (1904–1950), surgeon and pioneer in development of blood banks

Your teacher will help you select an important inventor or scientist from the middle part of the twentieth century for research and report writing.

LEARNING STRATEGY

Reminder: When you look for information on a topic, you are **using resources**. You can find these resources in your school or public library and on the Internet. Use this learning strategy when you need more information than what is in your textbook.

Hedy Lamarr (1914–2000), movie star, inventor of a torpedo guidance system that was forerunner of secure military communications

RESEARCHING Finding the Information You Need

1. Look for information about the inventor or scientist you have chosen. You may want to use biographies, an encyclopedia, and the Internet.

2. As you read, take notes on the important information about the person. Write your notes on index cards. Use a new card for each source. Use your own words, except when noting quotations that you think are important. (Look in Unit 1, page 26, for information about how to write direct quotations.) You need to find the following information: complete name, date of birth (and death, if no longer living), early years and education, occupation, accomplishments, and major contributions (why this person is important in U.S. history).

3. Look over your note cards. Do you need any more information?

WRITING A FIRST DRAFT Putting the Information Together

1. Use your note cards to make an outline of your report. Complete the outline form below on a separate sheet of paper. Add more items if necessary.

> [TITLE OF REPORT]
>
> **I.** Introduction
>
> Tell what your report will be about by giving the name of the person and why he or she is important.
>
> **II.** Early Life
>
> A. Date of birth and family background
> B. Education
> C. Family
>
> **III.** Accomplishments
>
> A. What was outstanding about this person?
> B. Did this person make a difference in the lives of others? How?
> C. Are this person's contributions still in use today?
>
> **IV.** Conclusion
>
> Give a brief summary of the important facts in your report. Then tell why your inventor or scientist is important in U.S. history.

2. When you complete your outline, you are ready to begin writing the first draft of your report. If possible, use a computer. This makes it easier to make revisions later.

Checking the Information in the Report

1. Read through your report. Does it have all the important information about your inventor or scientist? Add anything that is missing.

2. Read through your report again. Have you repeated any information? Is there information that is not important to your report? If so, take it out.

3. Now read your report out loud to a classmate. Is there something interesting you forgot to say? Ask for feedback, and take notes.

4. Now listen to your classmate's report. Give feedback that is helpful. If you are curious about something in your classmate's report, ask questions.

LEARNING STRATEGY

Discussing your report with others can help you make improvements. When you work with someone else, what learning strategy are you using?

EDITING **Checking Spelling, Punctuation, and Grammar**

1. Carefully check the spelling in your report. If you are using a computer, use the spell-check feature. Then reread carefully—the spell-check feature will not correct all errors! For instance, if you wrote *red* when you really meant *read* (past tense), the spelling checker will not correct it. Correct all spelling mistakes. Use a dictionary if necessary.

2. Now check for punctuation and capitalization. Does every sentence start with a capital letter? Do all names of places and people start with capital letters? Do all sentences end with a period, a question mark, or an exclamation mark? Are there commas between clauses in long sentences? Did you use quotation marks before and after quotes? Did you indent each paragraph? Correct any errors.

3. Now check the grammar. Remember to check the following:

   • Present tense, third-person singular ends in "-s" (she say<u>s</u>)

   • Adjectives come before nouns (a <u>poor</u> family)

   • Most verbs in a biographical report will be in the <u>past</u> tense (He <u>began</u> writing about his ideas when he was still in college.)

   • Check with your teacher if you are not sure about grammar.

4. Read your report one last time. Are you satisfied? Is it the best work you can do? If so, turn it in to your teacher.

PRESENTING AN ORAL REPORT

Sit in a small group with three other classmates. Read your reports to one another. Be ready to answer questions after reading your report. In your notebook, write three important things that you learned from listening to each classmate's report.

Three Presidents: 1940–1960

Only three presidents served from 1940 until 1960. Franklin Delano Roosevelt was elected four times, although he did not live to complete his fourth term. He was president for twelve years altogether. Today, there is a law limiting presidents to just two terms, or eight years.

PRESIDENT	EVENTS
1940	
Franklin Delano Roosevelt	1941 – Japanese attack on Pearl Harbor United States in World War II (1941–1945)
	1944 – D-Day invasion
1945 Harry S Truman	1945 – Roosevelt dies; Harry S Truman becomes president United States drops atomic bombs on Hiroshima and Nagasaki World War II ends
	1947 – Truman Doctrine (containment of communism) Marshall Plan in Europe
	1948 – Berlin airlift
	1949 – Soviet Union has the A-bomb
1950	
Dwight D. Eisenhower	1954 – *Brown v. Board of Education*, Supreme Court decision Senator Joseph McCarthy censured by Senate; ends anti-communist campaign
1955	1955 – Korean War ends United States begins to train South Vietnamese army
	1955–1956 – Montgomery, Alabama, bus boycott
	1956 – Eisenhower begins interstate highway system Montgomery bus boycott (1955–1956)
	1957 – *Civil Rights Act* President Eisenhower sends federal troops to integrate Little, Rock, Arkansas, school Soviet Union launches *Sputnik* Growth of computer use in industry (1954–1957)
1960	1960 – John F. Kennedy elected president (took office 1961)

Franklin Delano Roosevelt

Harry S Truman

Dwight D. Eisenhower

Using a Time Line

The presidential time line shows some of the events that happened during the terms of U.S. presidents between 1940 and 1960.

Work with a group of two or three classmates to construct a detailed time line of one of the three presidents who served between 1940 and 1960. Include information from the unit readings. Look up new information on the presidential time line in reference books or on the Internet so that you understand each event. Be sure that you include the inventions and the changes in technology during that time.

Present your detailed time line about one president to the rest of the class. As you listen to the presentations about the other presidents, take careful notes so that you can remember the information.

LIFE IN THE 1950S

Give each picture a title. Then write a paragraph that compares and contrasts these family scenes with family scenes you see today.

Eras of Protest: 1960–1980

Tell what you think

The period from 1960 to 1980 was a time of challenge and change in the United States. Different groups of people and individuals took their concerns to the courts, to the streets, or to television and newspapers to improve life for themselves, their families, and their country.

Look at the posters on these two pages. They show people and events from 1960 to 1980. What do you know about them? Why do you think these people and events were important? Do any of these images remind you of events happening now in the United States or in other countries?

Write your ideas in your notebook.

In this unit you will

- learn about new frontiers and Cold War events
- find out about the movements for civil rights
- learn about the ideas of civil disobedience, boycotts, and passive resistance
- find out about the Vietnam War
- discuss the ideas of five presidents
- use maps and charts
- research and write reports
- make oral presentations
- use time lines to learn about people and events

THE NAACP HAS BEEN FIGH
FOR FREEDOM FOR OVER 6
IT WASN'T EASY.
IT STILL ISN'T.

You can help. For information about our Special Contribution Fund
NAACP branch nearest you or write to: NAACP, SCF, 1790 Broadw

somebody paid the price
for your right

WE DEMAND AN END TO BIAS NOW!

register/vote

TIME LINE

1959
U.S. advisers in Vietnam

1960

1962–1968
College teach-ins
and demonstrations

1966
National Organization
for Women established

1968
American Indian
Movement established

1972
Watergate

1974
Nixon resigns

1979
Iran hostage crisis

1965

1970

1975

1980

1964
Freedom
summer

1968
United Farm Workers
established

1973
U.S. troops
leave Vietnam

1975
Vietnam
War ends

1979
Middle East peace settlement
(Camp David Accords)

Vocabulary

You will need to understand the meanings of these words and terms to understand the first part of this unit (pages 94–106). Use the Glossary to find the meanings of these words. Then write the words and their meanings in your notebook, using your own words. Do not copy the glossary definitions.

integrate	exile (n.)	sit-in	protest (n. and v.)
migrant worker	crisis (pl. crises)	segregation	intern (v.)
integration	confrontation	voting bloc	confront
internment	civil rights	advocate (v.)	

A New Frontier

For some groups of people in the United States, the 1960s began badly. In the South, African Americans were not allowed to vote. They were not attending integrated schools, even though the Supreme Court decision in 1954 (*Brown v. Board of Education*) gave them this right. Most Native Americans were living in poverty on reservations that were located on some of the poorest land in the country. Many Mexican Americans were working as day laborers or as migrant farmers who moved from south to north, harvesting the crops of the large farms for low wages. Japanese Americans who had lost businesses and land during their World War II internment were also struggling to improve their lives. Women, whose wartime factory jobs had paid them good wages, left those jobs when men returned from the war.

> *"And so, my fellow Americans: ask not what America will do for you, but what together we can do for the freedom of man."*
>
> —*President John F. Kennedy, Inaugural Address, January 20, 1961*

Some women stayed at home to raise families; others found work, but in lower-paying jobs.

As President John F. Kennedy took office in January 1961, many believed that he—a young (forty-two) and energetic man—would change things for the better. He talked about a "new frontier" of ideas to improve the lives of the poor, help the economy, and expand the space exploration program. Kennedy asked citizens to take responsibility for making the United States better. He inspired people and gave them hope.

What Do You Think?

In the early history of the United States, the *frontier* was the land in the western part of the country where people from the East moved to settle. People then thought of the frontier as a new land where they could make a better life for themselves and their families.

What do you think the "new frontier" meant in the 1960s?

Work with one or two classmates. Discuss your ideas and write them in your notebook. Then share your ideas with the class.

Thinking about what you have already learned about a topic gets you ready to learn more about the same topic. What is the name of this learning strategy?

LEARNING STRATEGY

Work with a partner. What have you already learned about the Cold War? Why was it called a "cold" war? Which countries were involved in this war? What were their major disagreements? What was the U.S. policy of containment? Write what you know in your notebook. Share your ideas with the class.

The Cold War Intensifies

THE BERLIN WALL

In the summer of 1961, without any warning, the Soviets began to build a wall across the city of Berlin and a barrier across Germany. Anyone trying to cross into the western part of Berlin was in danger of being shot by Soviet soldiers, but still many people tried to get over or under the wall. The Berlin Wall would divide families and friends for the next twenty-eight years. The wall symbolized to the whole world that there was a division between the East (the Soviet Union and its allies) and the West (the United States and its allies). Both sides also had the terrible power of the A-bomb. Both countries wanted to influence the rest of the world to choose their side, either democracy (the United States) or communism (the Soviet Union).

THE CUBAN CRISES

Several Cold War crises occurred in Cuba. This island nation, only about ninety miles from the United States, changed its government in 1959 when Fidel Castro led a successful revolt and overthrew the Cuban dictator Juan Batista. To assist Castro's government, the Soviet Union gave Cuba money, military equipment, and training for its army. This made Americans very uncomfortable about the threat of communism so close to their shores.

The United States tried several ways to isolate Cuba or change its communist government. Many Cubans who were against communism left Cuba after Castro came to power and lived as exiles in the United States. In 1961, the United States supported an invasion by about 1,300 of these Cuban exiles at the Bay of Pigs. The United States was sure that many anti-Castro Cubans would join the Cuban exiles to overthrow the Castro government. However, the invasion failed, and ninety people were killed and the rest captured. Castro remained in power.

A West Berliner walks along the wall in 1962.

There was a second confrontation between the United States and Cuba in 1962. The United States discovered that the Soviets had placed missiles in Cuba, and these were a great danger to the United States. For thirteen days in October, the United States and the Soviet Union had a "war of words" and the United States demanded that the Soviet Union remove the missiles. The Cuban Missile Crisis brought the United States and the Soviet Union very close to nuclear war. The United States prepared for a war. The United States used the Navy to prevent any more Soviet ships from bringing missiles to Cuba. This is called a *blockade*. At the last moment, the Soviet Union and the United States reached an agreement. The Soviet Union removed the missiles after the United States promised never to invade Cuba. Nuclear war was avoided.

The United States still refuses to trade or have diplomatic relations with Cuba. Many of those who came from Cuba as exiles are now U.S. citizens living in Florida. Some of them have continued to work to overthrow Castro, while others believe that the United States should have normal business and diplomatic relations with Cuba.

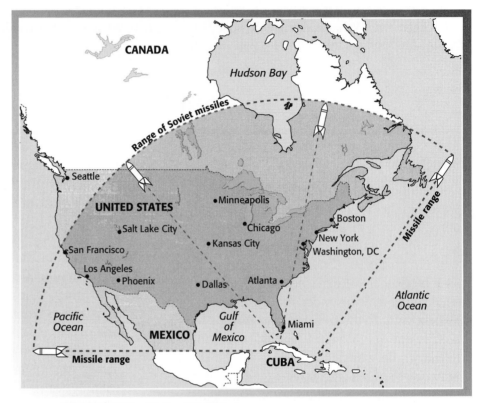

CRISES IN CUBA

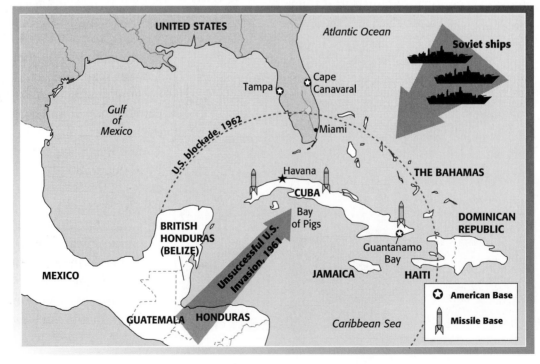

Missile sites in Cuba photographed by a U2 spy plane

The Space Race

The Cold War not only caused crises but also led to some important accomplishments for the United States. In 1957, the Soviets amazed the world by putting *Sputnik*, the first satellite, into orbit around the Earth. The United States hurried to catch up, and soon the two countries were competing in the exploration of space. This competition became known as the Space Race. President Kennedy announced a plan to be the first country to put a man on the moon by the end of the decade. The exploration of space became a "new frontier." He asked for and received from Congress more money to pay for the race to the moon.

The National Aeronautics and Space Administration (NASA), formed in 1958 by President Eisenhower, led the way. Although President Kennedy did not live to see the end of this race, the United States was the first country to successfully land a man on the moon. In July 1969, astronaut Neil Armstrong became the first person to walk on the moon. Millions of people around the world watched on television as Armstrong stepped onto the moon and said, "That's one small step for man; one giant leap for mankind."

The Apollo 11 rocket blasts off.

Neil Armstrong's photo of his co-pilot Edwin Aldrin walking on the moon.

THE PEACE CORPS

Another important outcome of the Cold War policies was Kennedy's establishment of the Peace Corps in 1961. President Kennedy had asked American people to serve others. He believed that it was important to help countries economically and to do so by people-to-people assistance. The Peace Corps is a program in which Americans volunteer to serve for two years in another country as health workers, agricultural or environmental specialists, or teachers. Between 1961 and 1963 more than 5,000 volunteers worked in more than forty countries. Since 1961, more than 165,000 Americans have been Peace Corps volunteers.

A Peace Corps volunteer works with local men on an irrigation canal in Nepal.

A Peace Corps volunteer works with students in British Honduras (Belize).

UNDERSTANDING WHAT YOU READ Comparing and Contrasting

In your notebook, draw a chart like the one below. Work with a classmate to complete your chart with information from "The Cold War Intensifies" selection.

POSITIVE RESULTS OF THE COLD WAR	NEGATIVE RESULTS OF THE COLD WAR	REASONS WHY POSITIVE OR NEGATIVE

LEARNING STRATEGY

When you use a chart, diagram, time line, or web to help you understand new information, what learning strategy are you using?

**LEARNING
STRATEGY**

You can understand new information better when you think back about related information that you have already studied. What is the name of this learning strategy?

Work with two or three classmates. Talk about what you have studied about the civil rights of different groups of Americans, including African Americans, Native Americans, Hispanic Americans, Asian Americans, and women. What do you already know about prejudice, violence, discrimination, protests, sit-ins, segregation, integration, and laws passed in the 1950s? After you talk about what you already know, discuss what you would like to learn about what happened to these groups in the 1960s and 1970s.

In your notebook, make a *K-W-L-H* chart like the model below. Write sentences to complete the *K* (What We Already *K*now) column. Write questions to complete the *W* (What We *W*ant to Find Out) column. You will complete the *L* and *H* columns later.

K	W	L	H

The Civil Rights Movement

The successes of government programs to contain communism and to do better than the Soviets in space were only part of the story of the 1960s. Many Americans of all ethnic groups celebrated the accomplishments of the United States in the Space Race. But the government would be challenged to do more. It would be asked to examine the differences in the way laws were applied to various ethnic groups. Different groups of people would use a variety of ways to gain the attention of the government and to demand equal rights. Much of this story took place in the 1960s and 1970s.

AFRICAN AMERICANS CONTINUE THEIR STRUGGLE FOR CIVIL RIGHTS

African Americans were the largest minority in the United States in the 1960s. Their struggle for greater freedom was very difficult. The ways they worked to gain the rights they had been guaranteed in the Constitution tells us an important part of America's story. The 1960s is one of the most important decades to study how the Constitution works for *all* people.

Anti-discrimination laws in the 1950s made it illegal to have separate schools, public buildings, or seating on public transportation for blacks and whites. But in many ways, especially in the South, whites continued to deny rights to blacks because they did not believe that African Americans should have the same rights as whites.

PEACEFUL PROTEST

A successful bus boycott in Montgomery, Alabama, in 1954–1955 led to the increased use of peaceful, non-violent protests. Sit-ins, marches, and demonstrations were also used to change unfair laws. For example, in early 1960, four African American college students sat down at a lunch counter in a Woolworth's store in Greensboro, North Carolina. The waiter refused to serve them. They remained seated, waiting for service, until the store closed for the night. They returned each day for six months, sometimes with many other students, until finally they were served.

The actions of these students did two things: They made the store follow the law and

Sit-ins often brought violent reactions from whites, as in Jackson, Mississippi, in 1963.

Martin Luther King, Jr., speaking to thousands, August 1963, Washington, DC

serve all customers, and they provided an example of how to make change peacefully. Other sit-ins followed.

Although there were many brave people involved in the civil rights movement, the Reverend Martin Luther King, Jr., was the best-known leader. He believed in the laws of the United States and that non-violence was the way to defeat segregation and racism. He led many of the marches and protests. He was arrested many times and spent time in jail, but he continued to preach peace. Thousands of people admired his ideas and followed his leadership.

Throughout the 1960s, there were many protests to increase the public's awareness of widespread discrimination against blacks in the United States. In one form of protest, called *freedom rides*, both black and white people traveled together across the South on buses to demonstrate against segregation on transportation. Others demonstrated by marching. In 1963 in Birmingham, Alabama, peaceful marchers were attacked by an angry mob of whites, including some police officers who used dogs and fire hoses to drive the marchers back. Freedom riders were stopped and their bus set on fire. Civil rights marchers and riders were injured in the attacks, and increasing violence led to the murders of several civil rights workers.

These incidents were reported in the news, and people across the country saw and read about them. They were shocked by the violence and began to

A Freedom Rider bus was bombed near Anniston, Alabama, in May 1961. The bus had stopped because of a flat tire. Passengers escaped without serious injury.

support the protesters and their goals.

A result of the non-violent actions of the civil rights movement was the passage of a new civil rights bill in 1964 that strongly enforced anti-discrimination laws in housing, education, transportation, and voting. This became a powerful symbol of the influence of non-violence creating change.

Malcolm X during a Black Muslim rally in New York, 1963

THE BLACK POWER MOVEMENT

Others who wanted change did not believe non-violence was the only way to get it. Men such as Malcolm X, Stokely Carmichael, and H. Rap Brown had other ideas. The Black Power movement came from their ideas. It focused on self-help, such as establishing businesses run by blacks and electing black officials. The followers of this movement challenged the government if it did not move quickly to enforce civil rights laws. They encouraged blacks to take pride in their African heritage and culture and advocated for the inclusion of African American history and culture in schools and universities. One way

groups expressed their pride was to choose the name by which they would be called. *Negro* was abandoned in favor of *black,* then *African American.*

MARTIN LUTHER KING, JR., IS ASSASSINATED

In spite of the peaceful, non-violent ways of Martin Luther King, Jr., and others, the 1960s was also a decade of violence. Martin Luther King, Jr., was assassinated in April 1968, and the nation mourned. Riots followed in many cities, such as Los Angeles, Newark, and Detroit, where many African Americans remained poor. The destruction from the riots focused attention on the terrible conditions in which many African Americans lived. The struggles to change these conditions would continue into the next decades.

There were successes and failures in the movement to gain equality. Civil rights were strengthened for African Americans in the 1960s by protests that led to successful court cases and new laws by Congress. Many other groups seeking their rights would follow the ideas and the methods of these African American leaders.

UNDERSTANDING WHAT YOU READ | **Making a Chart**

Copy this chart in your notebook. Make twelve rows. Then use the information in "The Civil Rights Movement" to complete the missing information. Hint: You may also use information from Unit 3.

AFRICAN AMERICANS AND CIVIL RIGHTS

DATE	GOALS	PEOPLE	METHODS USED	RESULTS
1954	Provide equal education for African American children	Thurgood Marshall	Legislation: decision by Supreme Court	*Brown v. Board of Education*: Schools desegregated
1954–1956		Martin Luther King, Jr.		

Martin Luther King, Jr.

You will listen to a short biography about the Reverend Martin Luther King, Jr.

Copy the T-list below in your notebook. As you listen to his life story, take notes on the information using the T-List. The main ideas are written on the left. Write the details and examples on the right. After you listen, compare your notes with two or three classmates. Did you forget anything? If so, add it to your notes. Finally, use your notes to write in your own words what you learned about Martin Luther King, Jr. Use complete sentences and paragraphs.

LEARNING STRATEGY

What strategy will you use to decide what information to write down? What learning strategy will you use to write down the key ideas?

MAIN IDEAS	DETAILS AND EXAMPLES
A. Early life and ideas of Martin Luther King, Jr.	1. _____ 2. _____ 3. _____ 4. _____
B. The Montgomery bus boycott	1. _____ 2. _____ 3. _____
C. Non-violence in action	1. _____ 2. _____ 3. _____
D. Later life and murder of Martin Luther King, Jr.	1. _____ 2. _____ 3. _____
E. Why Martin Luther King, Jr., is important in U.S. history	1. _____ 2. _____

Look at the four headings in "Others Struggle for Equality." Then read the questions below. Under which heading do you think you will find the answer to each question? Write the heading titles in your notebook. Then scan to find the answers to the questions. Write the answers. You do not have to write complete sentences.

What learning strategy are you using when you try to find specific information in a reading?

LEARNING STRATEGY

1. When was the National Organization for Women established?

2. What was the American Indian Movement (AIM)?

3. Who was César Chavez?

4. What happened to Japanese Americans after World War II?

5. Why did people from Southeast Asia immigrate to the United States in the 1970s?

6. About how many Native American people were living in the United States in the 1960s?

7. What methods did women use to get equal rights with men?

8. What methods did Puerto Ricans and Cuban Americans use to get equal treatment?

Others Struggle for Equality

NATIVE AMERICANS

Native Americans had been working for their rights for many years. Since the beginning of U.S. history, the government made treaties and fought wars with the native peoples to gain land for the settlers. This struggle left many Native Americans living on the poorest land in the country with no way to make their lives better.

By the 1960s, there were about 800,000 Native Americans in the United States. More than half of them were living on reservations where living conditions were terrible. As the civil rights movement developed, Native Americans joined in with their own message. They did not wait for the government to help

them. Instead, they advocated Red Power, or pride in being tribal members.

They went to the courts and asked for money from the government as payment for the use of Native American land and the return of fishing rights. They formed the American Indian Movement (AIM) to protect the protesters. They even took over the island of Alcatraz in 1969 to get people to recognize their demands for their own rights. To bring further attention to their cause, they had sit-ins at the Bureau of Indian Affairs building in Washington, DC, in 1972; and at a trading post at Wounded Knee, Pine Ridge Reservation, South Dakota, in 1973. Protesters were often arrested, and some remained in jail for a long

Members of the Sioux tribe plant a U.S. flag on Alcatraz Island.

time for their actions. These protest actions by a small group of Native Americans made many people very proud to be Native American. More Native Americans began to research their own heritage.

People in the United States became aware of the terrible living conditions on the reservations. Congress passed a law in 1974 that recognized the concerns of the tribes. It gave more power to the tribes to make decisions about their own lives.

With these rights, Native Americans gained economic and political power. On some reservations, native people built casinos. This brought many visitors to the reservations, where they spent money. With the money earned by the casinos, Native American tribes could build new schools and public buildings on the reservations.

The money also allowed them to argue for their rights in the courts and Congress. Today native people are using the courts to gain payments for use of their tribal lands by businesses and to receive payment of the fees the U.S. government guaranteed to them.

ASIAN AMERICANS

During World War II, Japanese Americans were interned in camps and lost their property, even though many Japanese Americans fought courageously in the war. After the war, Japanese Americans began to work through the courts to reclaim their property or to be paid for it. Finally, in 1982, the government apologized for its great injustice to Japanese Americans. In 1988, Congress agreed to pay $20,000 to each interned Japanese American who was still alive.

Other Asians came to the United States throughout the 1970s and 1980s from China, Korea, and South East Asia (Cambodia, Laos, and Vietnam). They were fleeing wars in their countries. These refugees often entered the United States with little money, and most could not speak English. Often, the only jobs they could find did not pay much money. Many of these refugees, like immigrants before them, moved into areas of cities in which there were others from their countries who could help them.

These immigrants worked to learn English because they believed education was the way to a better life. In 1974, a case was brought to the Supreme Court for a group of non-English-speaking Chinese

A shopping mall sign in Los Angeles advertises in Spanish, English, and Korean.

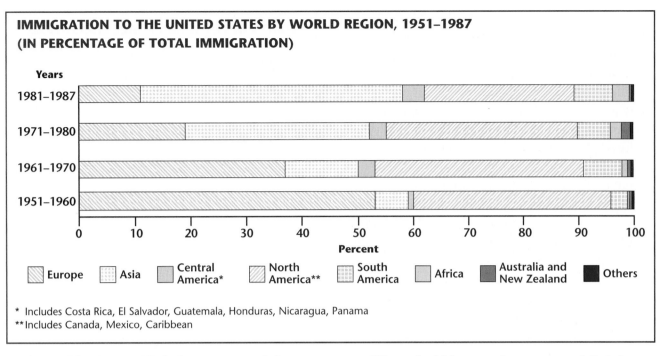

IMMIGRATION TO THE UNITED STATES BY WORLD REGION, 1951–1987 (IN PERCENTAGE OF TOTAL IMMIGRATION)

Years
1981–1987
1971–1980
1961–1970
1951–1960

Percent

Legend: Europe | Asia | Central America* | North America** | South America | Africa | Australia and New Zealand | Others

* Includes Costa Rica, El Salvador, Guatemala, Honduras, Nicaragua, Panama
**Includes Canada, Mexico, Caribbean

students. The *Lau v. Nichols* case argued that the Chinese students had an "unequal educational chance" because they had no way to learn English. The 14th Amendment to the Constitution (equal rights) was used to defend the argument. The Supreme Court agreed, and told the schools that they had to give students who were not native speakers of English special help to learn English. This ruling applied to all non-English-speaking students, not just those who spoke Chinese. After that, more schools began English as a Second language (ESL) and bilingual programs to help those students.

HISPANIC AMERICANS

The term *Hispanic* was first used in the 1970 U.S. Census, in which it was defined as any person who came from Central America, South America, or Spanish-speaking Caribbean nations. However, people from these areas of the world do not all have the same culture or even speak the same language. (For example, people from Brazil speak Portuguese.) Today, people whose families originally came from Spanish-speaking countries refer to themselves by many different names, such as Hispanic, Latino/a, Chicano/a, Puerto Rican, Mexican American, and Cuban American.

Hispanics' history of protests and fighting for equal rights is varied. César Chavez, a World War II veteran who wanted to help farm workers, led the strongest movement among Mexican Americans. In the 1960s, he formed the National Farm Workers Association in California, a union that seeks better working conditions for farmers. He called the struggle *La Causa* (The Cause). To protest farmers' bad working conditions, Chavez organized a strike of grape pickers and a nationwide boycott of grapes (and later lettuce) that had been picked by non-union workers. As a result of this protest, farm workers gained the right to negotiate their contracts.

César Chavez leads striking grape pickers in California

In addition to Chavez's work for farm laborers, the 1960s saw a Brown Power movement that was modeled on the African American Black Power movement. Organizations such as *Alianza* (Alliance) in New Mexico, *La Raza Unida* (The United People) in Texas, and the Crusade for Justice in Colorado worked at this time to give people more power over their own lives. Some demanded return of territory in the Southwest; some wanted Chicano/a studies at universities; others wanted to be consulted about decisions by the Immigration and Naturalization Service.

By 1970, almost 85 percent of Mexican Americans were living in urban areas. These Mexican Americans also became active in seeking rights. They worked to build pride in their backgrounds and to bring better education and health care to the poor in the cities. Like other groups, they worked in several ways to make these changes.

Most changes in the Hispanic community happened because people voted for politicians who promised to make changes. For example, the Puerto Rican population in New York City and the exiles from Castro's Cuba in Florida formed a large and vocal voting bloc. By the 1970s, people running for election were seeking votes from these Hispanic groups and were listening to what they wanted. Once elected, lawmakers voted to provide money for Puerto Rican neighborhoods in New York City and gave anti-Castro speeches in Florida. In Texas and California, there was a focus on how best to teach English to speakers of other languages and to instruct them on immigration laws. And in many of these areas, Hispanics ran for political office and won places on school boards and in local and state government.

WOMEN SEEK EQUALITY

Many things began to change for women in the 1960s. Some women wanted to work outside the home, but they found that either they could not get jobs or they were paid much less than a man who was doing the same job. Many women joined the civil rights movement in the 1960s, but found they were often doing

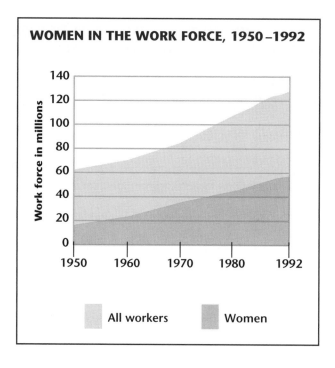

WOMEN IN THE WORK FORCE, 1950–1992

All workers · Women

the same jobs they did at home—making food or coffee for the leaders of the protests and cleaning up after their meetings.

In 1963, Betty Friedan wrote a book called *The Feminine Mystique*. This book challenged the idea that women could only be happy as wives and mothers. She founded the National Organization for Women (NOW) in 1966 to publicize women's ideas and goals for equality with men. To do this, women sometimes used the same non-violent methods that the civil rights leaders used. They held marches and spoke out for their rights to equality and a good education so that they could become doctors, lawyers, writers, or whatever they wanted, equal in pay and opportunity with men.

Women march along Fifth Avenue in New York, demanding equal rights.

1. Now meet with the same group of classmates you worked with to begin your *K-W-L-H* chart in the Before You Read activity on page 99. What new information have you learned about civil rights? What happened in the 1960s that made a difference in the lives of African Americans, Native Americans, Hispanic Americans, Asian Americans, and women?

2. Read what you wrote in the *K* (What We Already *K*now) column for the activity. Do you need to correct any facts that you listed? Do it now!

3. Read what you wrote in the *W* (What We *W*ant to Find Out) column. Were your questions answered? Check off the questions that were answered. Now, look for answers to the questions that still need to be answered. Use an encyclopedia or the Internet.

4. Now write sentences in the third column headed *L* (What We *L*earned) to tell what you learned about the civil rights movement in the 1960s and 1970s. A sample chart is shown below. Hint: You have already made a separate chart for African Americans (see page 101).

5. Talk with your classmates about how you learned the new information. Write the learning strategies that you used in the fourth column headed *H* (*H*ow We Learned).

6. Share your group's *K-W-L-H* chart with the rest of the class.

SAMPLE CHART FOR RECORDING WHAT YOU LEARNED

	LEADERS AND ORGANIZATIONS	GOALS	HOW DONE	RESULTS, DATES
African American	**Martin Luther King, Jr.** **Malcolm X** **Black Panthers**	**Voting rights** **Integration**	**Sit-ins** **Marches**	*Voting Rights Act*, 1965
Native American	**AIM** **Pelletier**	**Land rights**	**Sit-ins** **Political action**	
Hispanic	**Chávez** *La Raza*	**Education** **Immigration rights**	**Political action** **Strikes**	

LEARNING STRATEGY

Read the directions on the page. Then decide what learning strategy you will use to think, talk, or write about what you already know before you read new information. Write the name of the learning strategy.

Work with a classmate. Discuss what you know about Kennedy's presidency. What did he accomplish? What problems did he encounter and how did he try to solve them? Write your ideas in your notebook, and then share them with another pair of students.

End of an Era

THE DEATH OF PRESIDENT KENNEDY

On a clear, beautiful day in November 1963, President and Mrs. Kennedy got into a convertible for a trip, almost a parade, through downtown Dallas, Texas. As the motorcade rounded a curve, the president was shot. He was rushed to the local hospital, but he died. Vice President Lyndon Johnson was sworn in as president on *Air Force One*, the presidential airplane, as it flew him and Mrs. Kennedy back to Washington. The nation was in shock, and people mourned both in the United States and around the world. The man accused of shooting Kennedy, Lee Harvey Oswald, was himself shot as he was being led into the jail. The man who shot Oswald, Jack Ruby, was put in jail, but he died of cancer before he could be tried.

An investigation into the assassination of President Kennedy followed. It concluded that Oswald acted by himself to kill President Kennedy. Not everyone believed that conclusion and, to this day, there are people who continue to question who was responsible for President Kennedy's death.

Kennedy was president for less than three years, but he and his family remain very important to many people. He had many ideas about how to make peoples' lives

President and Mrs. Kennedy minutes before the assassination

better. He told Americans his ideas in his speeches. He and his wife and young children painted a picture of America that many people around the world admired.

President Kennedy did not live to see the development of his plans for improving people's lives, but the next president, Lyndon Johnson, made many of Kennedy's ideas happen.

"Let the word go forth from this time and place, to friend and foe alike, that the torch has been passed to a new generation of Americans . . . unwilling to witness or permit the slow undoing of those human rights to which this nation has always been committed, and to which we are committed today at home and around the world."
— *John F. Kennedy, Inaugural speech, January 20, 1961*

PRESIDENT JOHNSON AND THE GREAT SOCIETY

Like President Kennedy before him, President Lyndon B. Johnson saw a strong connection between poverty and civil rights. He believed that people were held back not just because of race and gender discrimination but also because of poverty. He realized that, especially in the cities, low wages or no jobs kept people in poverty. So President Johnson declared a "war on poverty." He worked to make lives better for many people by encouraging Congress to pass a series of laws.

More than a dozen major laws were passed between 1964 and 1966 to provide money and programs for Johnson's war on poverty. In 1964, the *Economic Opportunity Act* was passed. It included programs such as Head Start for preschool children and Volunteers in Service to America (VISTA) for volunteers to work in poor neighborhoods. The *Civil Rights Act* of 1964 banned discrimination in any federal program.

> *"There was no child we could not feed, no adult we could not put to work, no disease we could not cure, no toy, food, or appliance we could not make safer, no air or water we could not clean."*
> —*Johnson presidential aide*

The *Voting Rights Act* of 1965 extended voting rights to all Americans of all races. Bills passed in 1966 provided money for schools, low-income housing, and medical care for older people. They ended immigration quotas and funded the arts. Some cities got new public buildings and mass transit systems. Congress also passed federal safety standards for automobiles and tires, food and drugs.

At the same time, however, the United States was also fighting in Southeast Asia. The war, in which the United States had been involved since 1959, began to cost more money and more lives. By 1968, many of the programs Johnson had started failed.

HISTORY MYSTERY

What did Martin Luther King, Jr., mean when he said that Johnson's war on poverty was "shot down in the fields of Vietnam"?

UNDERSTANDING WHAT YOU READ Summarizing

LEARNING STRATEGY

When you write down the most important ideas in a reading text using your own words, what learning strategy are you using?

Write one or two sentences that express the main ideas in each section of "End of an Era." Write your summary in your notebook. Check it with a classmate. Did you answer these questions in your summary?

1. How did President Kennedy die?

2. What problems remained for President Johnson?

3. How did President Johnson want to help people?

4. Why was President Johnson unable to help people as much as he wanted?

BEFORE YOU READ **Using Maps to Make Predictions**

Study the map carefully. You may work with a classmate. Use the map to answer the questions and make predictions about the Vietnam War. Write your predictions in your notebook.

1. Which country would probably help North Vietnam with equipment and supplies? Why?

2. How do you think U.S. troops traveled to Vietnam?

3. How do you think U.S. troops got supplies and equipment?

4. Vietnam is in what geographical region? Why would this make ground fighting difficult?

5. The Vietnam War lasted from 1959 to 1975. Why do you think this war went on for so many years?

6. During the Vietnam War there was a draft. This meant that all young men in the United States from the age of eighteen could be forced to serve in the armed forces. How do you think young people reacted to this?

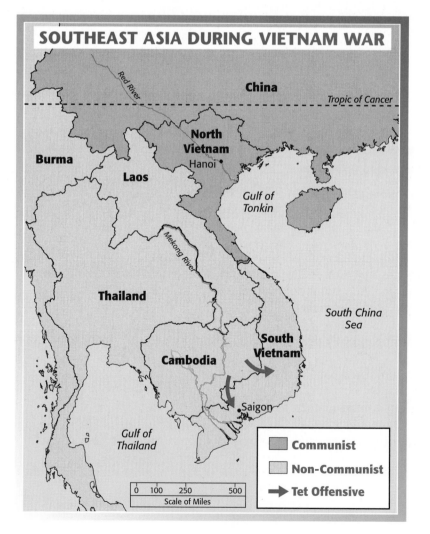

SOUTHEAST ASIA DURING VIETNAM WAR

The United States in Vietnam

U.S. troops in the Mekong Delta, South Vietnam, 1967

A peace agreement between France and Vietnam in 1954 had divided Vietnam into two parts. The North was headed by Ho Chi Minh, who was a communist, while the South was non-communist. The United States became involved in the Vietnam War because of the U.S. policy of containment. The United States feared that the other nations in the area (Cambodia, Laos, and South Vietnam) would become communist. In the late 1950s, the United States secretly began to help the non-communist South with military advisers and aid.

In 1964, the United States said that the North Vietnamese had attacked U.S. ships in the Gulf of Tonkin. The evidence was not clear but, by claiming that the United States had been attacked, President Johnson convinced Congress to pass the Gulf of Tonkin Resolution that gave Johnson the authority to send troops to Vietnam. By 1967, almost 500,000 U.S. troops were fighting an undeclared war in Southeast Asia.

ANTI-WAR PROTESTS

Unlike World War II, many people in the United States did not support this war. Students and faculty on college campuses and some newspaper reporters began to protest the involvement of the United States in Vietnam. Students occupied university buildings or attended "teach-ins," where they heard speeches against the war in Vietnam. Many students also marched and sang protest songs to show their feelings.

When Richard Nixon became president in 1969, he continued talks, begun in 1968, to end the war. Protests increased, however, and people questioned President Nixon's delay in ending the war. Most events were peaceful, until National Guard troops at Kent State University and highway patrolmen at Jackson State College in Mississippi shot and killed six students in 1970. By this time, almost 60 percent of the American people were against the war.

National Guardsmen use tear gas at Kent State University on May 4, 1970. Later, four students were shot and killed.

A Peace Agreement

The war and the peace talks went on for several more years. A cease-fire and peace agreement was finally reached in 1973. All sides agreed to release prisoners, and the United States agreed to withdraw its troops. There was no clear winner of the Vietnam War.

Americans were glad to have their troops coming home. North and South Vietnam continued to fight until April 1975, when the South surrendered to the North and Vietnam was united into one country. The loss of life on all sides was enormous. The names of the more than 58,000 Americans who lost their lives are written on the Vietnam Veterans Memorial in Washington, DC. In addition to those killed, 300,000 soldiers were wounded, listed as missing in action (MIA), or suffered illness or disability caused by the war.

A veteran mourns at the Vietnam Veterans Memorial in Washington, DC. The memorial was designed by 21-year-old Maya Lin.

The Vietnam War created a debate in the United States and other countries that continues today. This debate is about whether the United States has the right to interfere in the business of other nations. If so, what events should have to occur to allow the United States to interfere in another country?

UNDERSTANDING WHAT YOU READ **Checking Predictions**

Work with the same classmate that you worked with to make predictions about the Vietnam War. Check each prediction, and correct it, if necessary. If the information is not in the reading, check your school library or the Internet.

UNDERSTANDING WHAT YOU READ **Writing and Working with Study Questions**

1. Work with a partner. For each paragraph of the reading on the Vietnam War, write one or two questions that will help you study and remember the main information in that paragraph. Write your questions in your notebook.

2. With your partner, write answers to your study questions on a second sheet of paper. Keep this answer key.

3. Now exchange your questions with another pair of students. They have to write answers to your questions, and you and your partner have to write answers to their questions.

4. Now correct the answers that other students have written for your questions using the answers you wrote in item 2. They will also correct your answers.

5. Compare the results. What questions were the most difficult to answer? Why?

Read the vocabulary list with a classmate. If you already know some of these words, tell what they mean. Then skim "Protecting the Environment" to find how each word is used in context. Use the context to develop a definition for each new word. Write each word and its definition in your notebook. Check your definitions in the Glossary.

environment	nuclear plant
pest	fragile
emissions	endangered
pesticide	pollution
nuclear waste	conservation

Protecting the Environment

During the 1970s, many people in the United States were becoming concerned about the environment. Those in the movement to protect the environment used some of the same ways of organizing as did the civil rights groups, but it involved a very different subject—the Earth.

Silent Spring was an important book written by Rachel Carson in 1962. This book explained how chemicals, used to control harmful insects or pests, were polluting the water supply. As a result of this book, people began demanding laws that would make companies build factories and products that would not damage the water and air. These laws stated that cars and factories should have emission controls, that pesticides should be limited, and that nuclear plants should safely dispose of nuclear waste.

Laws were also passed to protect endangered animals and plants and to preserve the wilderness. The *Clean Air Acts*, which were first passed in 1963, set standards for factory and car emissions.

The Environmental Protection Agency (EPA) was established in 1970 to make sure that everyone followed the laws, and to suggest new laws.

People across the United States and around the world continue to speak and write against pollution and damage to the air we all breathe and the water we all drink. The first Earth Day celebration occurred in April 1970. It is celebrated annually as a way to remind everyone of the value of conservation of the Earth's resources and that there is still much to be done.

Demonstration on Earth Day, 1970

What types of pollution are mentioned in the reading? Which do you think are the most dangerous? Why? Do these kinds of pollution still exist today? What is being done about them?

Write a paragraph explaining your ideas. Hint: If you need additional information, consult reference books or the Internet.

Edit your paragraph carefully then share it with a classmate.

Understanding Songs of Protest

During the protests and marches of the civil rights movement and the Vietnam War, many popular songs were written and sung. These songs expressed the feelings of protest, despair, and hope that so many people were feeling.

Look up the *lyrics* (words) of some protest songs, such as "We Shall Overcome," "Blowin' in the Wind," and "The Times They Are a-Changing" on the Internet or in your library. What do they really mean? What ideas and emotions are they expressing? Discuss your ideas and understanding of these songs with two or three classmates. Then each group reports its ideas to the class.

Pete Seeger

Bob Dylan and Joan Baez

Woody Guthrie

Leaders of Change

In the 1960s and 1970s, ordinary men and women emerged as leaders of change. They inspired others to protest and to work on these changes in different ways. These leaders contributed to important movements that would affect many Americans.

Your teacher will help you select an important leader of change for research and report writing.

LEARNING STRATEGY

When you need information on a topic that is not in your textbook, where can you look? What learning strategy will you use?

Betty Friedan

Rachel Carson

Dolores Huerta and César Chavez

Rosa Parks

Rodolfo Gonzalez

S. I. Hayakawa

Dennis J. Banks

RESEARCHING Finding the Information You Need

1. Look for information about the leader you have chosen. You may want to use biographies, an encyclopedia, and the Internet.

2. As you read, take notes on the important information about the person. Write your notes on index cards. Use a new card for each source. Use your own words except when noting quotations that you think are important. You need to find the following information:

   - Complete name
   - Date of birth (and death, if no longer living)
   - Early years and education
   - Occupation
   - Ideas that inspired others
   - Accomplishments (changes this person made and how they were made)
   - Major contributions (why this person is important in U.S. history)

3. Look over your note cards. Do you need any more information?

WRITING A FIRST DRAFT Putting the Information Together

1. Use your note cards to make an outline of your report. Complete the outline form below on a separate sheet of paper. Add more items, if necessary.

> [TITLE OF REPORT]
>
> **I.** Introduction
>
> Tell what your report is about by giving the name of the person and why he or she is important.
>
> **II.** Early Life
>
> A. Date of birth and early years
> B. Education
> C. Family background
>
> **III.** Accomplishments
>
> A. What was outstanding about this person?
> B. Did this person make a difference in the lives of others? How?
> C. Are this person's contributions still used today?
>
> **IV.** Conclusion
>
> Give a brief summary of the important facts in your report. Then tell why the person you chose is important in U.S. history.

2. When you complete your outline, you are ready to begin writing the first draft of your report. If possible, use a computer. This makes it easier to make revisions later.

Checking the Information in the Report

1. Read through your report. Does it have all the important information about your leader of change? Add anything that is missing.

2. Read through your report again. Have you repeated any information? Is there information that is not important to your biography? If so, take it out.

3. Now read your report out loud to a classmate. Is there something interesting you forgot to say? Ask for feedback, and take notes.

4. Now listen to your classmate's report. Give feedback that is helpful. If you are curious about something in your classmate's report, ask questions.

LEARNING STRATEGY

Discussing your report with others can help you make improvements. When you work with someone else, what learning strategy are you using?

EDITING **Checking Spelling, Punctuation, and Grammar**

1. Carefully check the spelling in your report. If you are using a computer, use the spell-check feature. Then reread carefully—the spell-check feature will not correct all errors! For instance, if you wrote *red* when you really meant *read* (past tense), the spell checker will not correct it. Correct all spelling mistakes. Use a dictionary, if necessary.

2. Now check for punctuation and capitalization. Does every sentence start with a capital letter? Do all names of places and people start with capital letters? Do all sentences end with a period, a question mark, or an exclamation point? Are there commas between clauses in long sentences? Did you use quotation marks before and after quotes? Did you indent each paragraph? Correct any errors.

3. Now check the grammar. Remember to check the following:
   - Adjectives come before nouns (a <u>poor</u> family)
   - Most verbs in a biography will be in the past tense (He <u>began</u> writing about his ideas when he was still in college.)
   - Remember that many past tense verbs have irregular forms (wrote, spoke, sat, etc.)
   - Check with your teacher if you are not sure about grammar.

4. Read your report one last time. Are you satisfied? Is it the best work you can do? If so, turn it in to your teacher.

PRESENTING AN ORAL REPORT

Sit in a small group with three other classmates. Read your reports to one another. Be ready to answer questions after reading your report. In your notebook, write three important things that you learned from listening to each classmate's report. Then work with a classmate to make a graphic organizer for one of the reports you heard.

Vocabulary

To understand some of the problems from the late 1960s and throughout the 1970s, you need to know the meanings of the words in the box. In your notebook, write the word, then write the correct definition next to it.

accord
budget deficit
détente
hostage
inflation
interest rate
recession
strategic arms
tap telephones
unemployment

1. a relaxing of international tensions

2. an agreement

3. when people do not have jobs

4. to secretly listen in on the phone conversations of others

5. a prisoner who is held until a condition is met (such as payment of money, promise to stop fighting, admission of fault)

6. a situation in which there is not enough money to pay expenses

7. the percentage charged by banks as a fee when they lend money

8. military equipment that a country keeps in case of a war

9. when prices of goods and services rise too high

10. when business decreases, many are out of work, and the value of stocks goes down

Presidents Nixon, Ford, and Carter

NIXON: SUCCESS AND CRISIS IN THE PRESIDENCY

Presidents of the United States make decisions about issues both inside and outside the United States. Issues inside the country are called *domestic issues*, while issues that involve other nations are called *foreign policy*.

Richard Nixon became president in 1969 after Johnson's term was over. President Nixon had a number of foreign policy successes. He promoted a policy that was called *détente* (relaxing of international tensions), and it eased the strain between the United States and some communist countries. In 1972, he was the first president to travel to Communist China, and trade between the two countries started up for the first time since 1949. Nixon also visited the Soviet Union and arranged the SALT I (Strategic Arms Limitation Talks) agreement that limited the number of nuclear weapons built by the United States and the Soviet Union.

These two countries also agreed to work together in space and on health programs. After

President Nixon in China

two wars between Israel and some Arab nations, Nixon worked with Arab nations and Israel to build a better relationship. The United States needed oil from the Middle East and did not want Arab nations to become communist.

However, President Nixon was not successful in domestic policy. There was a budget deficit, high unemployment, and inflation. He did not like the groups who worked against the war in Vietnam or fought for civil rights. He used government organizations to check peoples' tax records and to "tap" telephones (listen in on conversations). When the FBI (Federal Bureau of Investigation) refused to do some of the things Nixon asked, he created a secret group in the White House to carry out his orders.

As President Nixon campaigned for re-election in 1972, his secret group tried to break into the office of the Democratic party in the Watergate Hotel in Washington, DC. They were caught. Nixon said that he knew nothing about it, but soon it was clear that he had lied. The fact that a president had lied to the American people created a huge scandal. Finally, in 1974, Nixon had to resign as president. He became the first and only president of the United States to resign his office.

PRESIDENTS GERALD FORD AND JIMMY CARTER

Nixon had appointed Gerald Ford to be vice president after Nixon's first vice president (Spiro Agnew) resigned because of corruption charges. When Nixon resigned, Ford became the new president. Ford was the only man to become president by being appointed, instead of being elected as vice president first. President Ford governed a country that had many problems. For example, there was a recession, high unemployment, and the price of gasoline was also very high. Internationally, President Ford met with the leader of the Soviet Union and they began work on a new nuclear arms limitation treaty, SALT II. No decision was made, however, and discussions continued through the next two presidencies.

Egyptian President Anwar Sadat, President Carter, and Israeli Prime Minister Menachem Begin sign the Camp David Accords, March 26, 1979.

President Jimmy Carter took office in January 1977. The problems that President Ford had tried to solve continued. Carter tried to revive the U.S. economy. He also worked with other nations to try to build peace in the Middle East. The Camp David Accords between President Anwar Sadat of Egypt and Prime Minister Menachem Begin of Israel were a start to peace. Other nations in the Middle East did not agree. In 1979, fifty Americans were taken hostage in Iran following a revolution in that country. These Americans would remain hostages for over a year.

In the election of 1980, the United States had an inflation rate of more than 10 percent, interest rates of 20 percent, and an unemployment rate of 8 percent. Americans liked Carter but were not happy with his ideas. They voted against him, and in 1980 they elected Ronald Reagan.

UNDERSTANDING WHAT YOU READ **Developing a Study Chart**

You have read about the three presidents who followed Lyndon Johnson. Work with a partner. Copy this chart in your notebook and complete it with information about each president.

PRESIDENT	DOMESTIC EVENTS/PROBLEMS	FOREIGN EVENTS/PROBLEMS
Richard Nixon		
Gerald Ford		
Jimmy Carter		

Five Presidents: 1960–1980

Five presidents served from 1960 to 1980. John F. Kennedy was elected in 1960 and assassinated in 1963. His vice president, Lyndon Johnson, became president, completed Kennedy's term, and won the 1964 election. Richard Nixon was elected twice, Gerald Ford completed Nixon's term, and Jimmy Carter served one term only.

PRESIDENT	EVENTS
–1960	**1960 – Sit-ins in Greensboro, North Carolina**
	Student Nonviolent Coordinating Committee (SNCC) formed
John F. Kennedy	1961 – Bay of Pigs
	Berlin Wall erected by Soviets
	Congress of Racial Equality (CORE) organizes Freedom Rides
	Interstate Commerce Commission (ICC) bans segregation on interstate transportation.
	1962 – Cuban missile crisis
	Peace Corps established
	The first black student enters University of Mississippi
	Malcolm X speaks for a separate black nation in the United States
Lyndon B. Johnson	1963 – Rev. Martin Luther King, Jr., "I Have a Dream" speech
	President Kennedy assassinated
	Lyndon B. Johnson becomes president
	1964 – *Civil Rights Act*
	Bay of Tonkin Resolution
	24th Amendment ratified
	1964–1966 War on Poverty
–1965	**1965 – Rev. King leads march for voter registration in Alabama**
	Voting Rights Act
	Malcolm X assassinated
	1965–1970 Anti-war protests
	1966 – Black Panthers formed
	1968 – *Fair Housing Act*
	Tet Offensive in Vietnam
	Martin Luther King, Jr., assassinated
Richard M. Nixon	1969 – First Americans on moon

John F. Kennedy

Lyndon B. Johnson

–1970		1970 – Students killed at Kent State and Jackson State Universities
–		
–		1972 – Watergate break-in
–		1973 – U.S. troops leave Vietnam
–	Gerald Ford	1974 – Nixon resigns
		Gerald Ford becomes president
–1975		
–		
–	Jimmy Carter	
–		
–		1979 – Peace treaty between Egypt and Israel
		Accident at Three Mile Island nuclear power plant
		Restored relations with People's Republic of China
		Iran takes U.S. hostages
–1980		1980 – Carter stops SALT II talks
		Soviets invade Afghanistan
		United States boycotts Olympic Games in Moscow

UNDERSTANDING WHAT YOU READ | Constructing a Time Line

The presidential time line shows some of the events that happened during the terms of U.S. presidents between 1960 and 1980. Some of the events listed include information that was not in the unit readings. Some of the events in the readings are not on the time line.

Work with a group of two or three classmates to construct a detailed time line of one of the five presidents that served between 1960 and 1980. Include information from the unit readings. Look up new information on the presidential time line in reference books or on the Internet so that you understand the events.

Present your time line about one president to the rest of the class. As you listen to the presentations about the other presidents, take careful notes so that you can remember the information.

Gerald Ford and Richard Nixon

Jimmy Carter

The American Identity: 1980 to the Present

The United States has been a nation for more than 200 years. Guided by the Constitution and the Bill of Rights, individuals and the government have made decisions, both good and bad, that together make up a complete picture of the nation.

In this unit you will learn about the end of the 20th and the beginning of the 21st centuries. This unit will also help you think about the future. What will be the next chapter in the story of the United States of America?

Tell what you think

As in other times, since 1980 there have been events of great triumph and tragedy. What do you know about the events pictured here? Are there other events you would include? Why?

Write your ideas in your notebook.

In this unit you will

- find out information about local and state governments
- learn about government decisions in a changed world
- examine technological changes
- learn about the presidents since 1980
- listen to biographical information
- research and write a report
- use maps, charts, and graphs; interpret political cartoons and photographs
- use evidence to make predictions

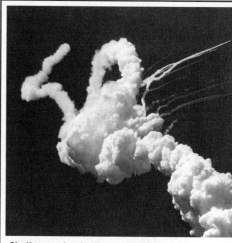

Challenger shuttle disaster, 1986

Hubble telescope photograph, 1995

TIME LINE   1980

1981
Ronald Reagan
becomes president

Alfred P. Murrah Federal Building in Oklahoma City bombed, 1995

UN peacekeepers in Bosnia, 1998

New Yorkers flee the World Trade Center, September 11, 2001

Exxon Valdez oil spill cleanup, 1989

Gulf War, 1991

American bald eagle no longer endangered, 1999

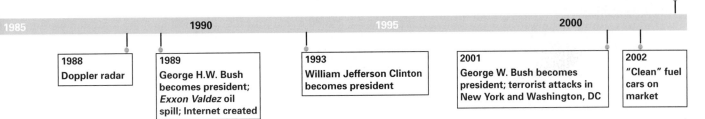

2003
Shuttle *Columbia* explodes; Gulf War II

1985 1990 1995 2000

1988
Doppler radar

1989
George H.W. Bush becomes president; *Exxon Valdez* oil spill; Internet created

1993
William Jefferson Clinton becomes president

2001
George W. Bush becomes president; terrorist attacks in New York and Washington, DC

2002
"Clean" fuel cars on market

Identifying What You Already Know

Read the directions on the page. Then decide what learning strategy you will use to think, talk, or write about what you already know about the topic before you read new information about it. Write the name of the learning **LEARNING STRATEGY** strategy in your notebook.

Work with a classmate. Discuss the two questions below. Write your ideas in your notebook. Share your ideas with the rest of the class.

1. Why do people and their families move from one place to another? Give at least three reasons.

2. You have learned about other times in U.S. history when people moved from one part of the country to another. When did these movements happen? Why did people move?

Jobs Change; People Move

SHIFT TO HIGH-TECH INDUSTRIES

Since the 1980s, large numbers of people in the United States have been on the move. There have been several reasons for these moves.

One reason was that factories in the Midwest began to lose business, so many people lost their jobs. Some of the factories moved to other states or outside the United States, where labor was cheaper. Some workers moved with their companies. But in many industries, like automobiles and steel production, machines and computers began to do more of the work.

People also moved because they found new job opportunities. In the 1980s, the production of computers became a large industry and created many new jobs. Many of the new high-tech industries were located in Silicon Valley, in California. This area became known as a center for the development of computer technology, and people with skills in computers moved there to be part of this growing industry.

While there were many new, high-skilled jobs, these jobs went to educated, highly skilled workers. New immigrants and workers with little or no education or skills took low-skilled,

FASTEST GROWING OCCUPATIONS, 2000–2010
(Numbers in thousands of jobs)

Occupation	2000	2010	Increase
Computer software engineers, applications	380	760	100%
Computer support specialists	506	996	97%
Computer software engineers, systems software	317	601	90%
Network and computer systems administrators	229	416	82%
Network systems and data communications analysts	119	211	77%
Desktop publishers	38	63	67%
Database administrators	106	176	66%
Personal and home care aides	414	672	62%
Computer systems analysts	431	689	60%
Medical assistants	329	516	57%

0   500,000   1,000,000

Source: Bureau of Labor Statistics, U.S Department of Labor, 2000.

lower-paying jobs, such as working in fast-food restaurants or doing custodial work in offices and buildings. In the past, these people might have gotten jobs in factories. But as factories were closing across the United States, many unskilled people were left unemployed or forced to accept poor wages.

Shift from the Cities to the Suburbs

For many people the move from the cities to the suburbs that began after World War II continued. Even if people worked at a job in the city, the houses they wanted to buy were outside the city. As more people moved outside the cities, building roads and mass transportation became important. Beginning in the late 1970s, cities such as San Francisco and Washington, DC, built subway systems to help ease traffic problems and reduce pollution. Other cities such as Chicago and New York had built subways in the 19th century, but they continued to build and expand their roads.

New subway systems linked the cities

UNDERSTANDING WHAT YOU READ Using Context

LEARNING STRATEGY

When you use context to help you understand new words, what learning strategy are you using? Write the name of the strategy in your notebook.

Work with a classmate. Discuss each of the following vocabulary words in "Jobs Change; People Move." What do you think each word means? Can you figure out the meaning from the context? Reread the selection, and write down your ideas in your notebook. Check your definitions in the Glossary.

low-skilled job	wages	custodial work
high-skilled job	high-tech industry	fast-food restaurant

AFTER YOU READ Finding Out More Information

You have read about low-skilled and high-skilled jobs. What are two differences between these two kinds of jobs?

Work with two or three classmates. Find out about low-skilled and high-skilled jobs in your own community. Look at the classified ads for employment in your local newspaper. What skills are needed for the high-skilled jobs? What skills are needed for the low-skilled jobs? What differences are there in wages for each type of job? What is your conclusion?

Share the information you find with the whole class.

Changes in where people lived and worked also caused changes in schools. As populations shifted, some new schools were built or old schools enlarged. In areas where jobs were lost, some schools were closed. School programs also changed because students had to learn new things. For example, schools began teaching students how to use computers. Many schools began or increased English classes for immigrant children.

What do you know about your own school? Work with a classmate. Discuss the questions below and write your answers in your notebook.

1. When was your school built? How has your school changed since it was built?

2. Who decides what subjects and textbooks you will study?

3. Who pays for books, supplies, computers, and other things you need?

4. What special programs does your school have (for example, English for Speakers of Other Languages [ESOL], special education, music, sports)?

Schools in the United States have changed in many ways since they began in the 1800s.

Schools Meet America's Changing Needs

The 10th Amendment of the U.S. Constitution says that any power not given to the federal government is reserved for the states and local communities. One of the most important powers held by the states is education. States decide things such as what kinds of schools to build, what rules students will follow, and what they will learn. States and local communities provide 80–90 percent of the money required to operate public schools.

Since there are more than 15,000 school districts in the United States, not all schools teach the same things. They respond to their communities and the economy in different ways. For example, when increased numbers of students from other countries come to an area, schools must find money to educate them. Schools also provide the latest knowledge and technology skills that students need for new kinds of jobs.

Many modern schools have students from every part of the world.

Individuals or groups who believe that they are not being treated fairly in the schools can ask the courts for help. Federal law overrules state law in the area of equal rights to an education.

How Schools are Changing

The states and cities pay for most of the costs of education. The federal government, however, also passes laws that require schools to create programs or test certain students. These new requirements cost money, and the federal government does not always provide funds to help states meet the laws' requirements.

What happens in schools and with students should reflect a balance between governmental policy and the voices of individuals, such as teachers, students, and parents, who are most involved in what schools do.

You have read about how schools in the United States operate in general. Each school system varies, however, because different communities and states organize their schools in different ways.

Go back to the questions in Before You Read (page 126). How can you check the answer for each question? Work with a group of classmates to investigate one of the questions. You will need to interview people at your school such as teachers, counselors, and the principal or assistant principal. When your group has found as much information as possible about your school, make a report to the whole class.

Find Out about Your State's Government

Much of U.S. history follows the lives and times of the presidents, but as you discovered in studying schools, there are also active governments in each of the fifty states and in the District of Columbia. The ideas and interests of people in California, Alabama, and Connecticut may be different for many reasons. Each state has a constitution, a leader (the governor), a legislature, and a supreme court.

Work in groups of four or five to find out information about the government of your state. Design a poster that shows how your state's government works. Be sure that your poster includes answers to the following questions:

1. What is the name of your state's governor, and where is his or her office?

2. How is a governor chosen, and how long can a governor stay in office?

3. What are the governor's main jobs? Who helps him or her?

4. When was your state constitution written, and what are its main ideas?

5. How is the legislature chosen, and what are its main responsibilities?

6. How is the state supreme court chosen, and what are its main responsibilities?

Share your poster with the whole class. After seeing all the posters in your class, your group should add any important information that was missing from your poster.

LEARNING STRATEGY What learning strategies did your group use to find the information about your state government and to design your poster? Did these learning strategies help you? How? Write your answers in your notebook.

HISTORY MYSTERY

British Prime Minister Winston Churchill said, "Democracy is the worst possible form of government—except for all the others." What did he mean?

The Sánchez Sisters

LISTENING AND TAKING NOTES

In addition to changes in jobs, places where people live, and schools, there have also been changes in government. More women and minorities are taking part in politics. You will listen to information about two sisters who have been elected to the U.S. House of Representatives—Loretta Sánchez and Linda Sánchez.

Linda Sánchez and Loretta Sánchez

Copy the T-list below in your notebook. As you listen, take notes on the information using the T-list below. The main ideas are written on the left. Write the details and examples on the right. After you listen, compare your notes with two or three classmates. Did you forget anything? If so, add it to your notes. Finally, use your notes to write in your own words what you learned about the Sánchez sisters. Use complete sentences and paragraphs.

LEARNING STRATEGY

What strategy will you use to decide what information to write down? What learning strategy will you use to write down the key ideas? Write them in your notebook.

MAIN IDEAS	DETAILS AND EXAMPLES
A. Early life and family background	1. _____ 2. _____ 3. _____ 4. _____
B. Education	1. _____ 2. _____ 3. _____
C. Running for political office	1. _____ 2. _____ 3. _____
D. Achievements in Congress	1. _____ 2. _____
E. Plans for the future	1. _____ 2. _____

What would the weather be like where you live if the average temperature was 10° F (5° C) higher than it is now? How would your life change in the summer? How would your life change in the winter?

Work with a partner to discuss your ideas. Write them in your notebook. Share your ideas with the rest of the class.

Environmental Concerns Increase

INCREASING POLLUTION

As the 20th century came to a close, people continued to worry about damage to the environment. Pollution was increasing because of the use of chemicals to kill farm insects and the increase in waste from nuclear weapons production and power plants, fumes from factories, and people's litter and trash. How much pollution could the Earth take before the environment was so damaged that it could not recover? This question made many people concerned about how life on Earth in the future might be affected.

Twenty million Americans took part in the first Earth Day. Thirty years later, Earth Day is still celebrated.

ENVIRONMENTAL ACCIDENTS

Two environmental accidents made many more people aware of the importance of protecting our environment. One of these accidents happened in 1979 at a nuclear power plant at Three Mile Island near Harrisburg, Pennsylvania. A small amount of radioactive gas escaped into the air, and many people who lived there abandoned their homes because they were afraid that their health might be affected. Another serious environmental accident happened in 1989, when the oil tanker *Exxon Valdez* had an accident off the coast of Alaska and spilled more than 10 million gallons of crude oil into the water. The oil damaged hundreds of acres of coastline and killed thousands of birds, animals, and fish.

earth day 2000

1970   celebrating 30 years of protecting new jersey's environment   2000

Earth Day poster, 2000

An oil-covered bird after the *Exxon Valdez* spill

GLOBAL WARMING

In 1992, Al Gore, a senator from Tennessee, wrote a book titled *Earth in the Balance*. This book described how our environment is changing and why we should protect the Earth. Later, as vice president from 1993–2001, Gore made the environment one of his major issues. In the 1990s, air pollution was exceeding the standards set by the federal government because many pollutants, such as carbon dioxide, were going into the air from cars and factories. The Environmental Protection Agency (EPA) reported that the ozone layer around the Earth that protects people from the Sun's rays was getting thinner and that this was causing *global warming*, or the gradual increase in average temperatures around the world.

Not everyone agrees that global warming is really happening or, if it is, that humans are responsible for it. In caring for the environment, there is always a search for a balance between the concerns of those who want to preserve the land, water, and air and those who need and use the Earth's minerals and energy. States are trying to preserve the cleanliness of their rivers, lakes, and air.

Industries need land and resources to grow. Nations around the world need to use their resources for growing populations. At the same time, damage to air and water in one part of the world eventually affects plants, animals, and people everywhere.

UNITED NATIONS ENVIRONMENTAL CONFERENCES

The United Nations has sponsored conferences about the environment. The role of the United States in environmental issues is important because it has many factories in this country and around the world. The United States also consumes a lot of the world's resources. Environmentalists continually work with the United States and with the United Nations to bring their concerns before the governments of the world.

In 1990, Congress passed a law to establish the *Clean Air Act*, but in 2002 the federal government weakened some of the clean air standards for factories and water. Clean air standards continue to be an issue that concerns governments, businesses, environmentalists, and people around the world.

UNDERSTANDING WHAT YOU READ **Environmental Issues in Your Community**

1. Work with a classmate. Make a graphic organizer or an illustrated poster that shows the most important environmental issues described in the reading.

2. Find out about your own town or city. Does it have any of the same environmental issues as those on your graphic organizer or poster? What are the concerns of environmentalists in your community? What are the environmental concerns of factories or businesses in your community? Make another graphic organizer or illustrated poster that shows the most important environmental issues in your town or city and how environmentalists and businesses are addressing them.

3. Discuss with the class actions that all of you can take to help keep your own environment clean. Write down at least three things you can do to help your own environment.

Looking for Specific Information

In your notebook, make a chart like the one below. As you read pages 131–133, choose one invention for each category and look for the answers to the five questions on the chart and write them in the correct boxes. You can review Units 1–4 to help you with Question 2. You need to use your own ideas to answer Questions 4 and 5.

LEARNING STRATEGY

What learning strategy will you be using when you scan a text to find specific information? Write it in your notebook.

INVENTIONS

	MEDICINE: _____	COMPUTERS: _____	TRAVEL: _____	COMMUNICATION: _____
1. Who uses this invention? How do they use it?				
2. What is another invention that is similar to this one?				
3. How did this invention change people's lives in the United States?				
4. What new invention do you predict will be based on this one?				
5. How might this new invention change people's lives in the future?				

Inventions Change Our Lives Again

In the last thirty years there have been many inventions in medicine, communications, the media, and transportation. Most of these inventions developed from earlier inventions and will probably lead to other new inventions. Although we cannot be sure what the next inventions might be, we can be sure of one thing: Inventions change our lives.

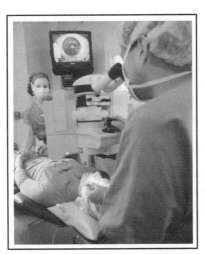

An eye surgeon performs laser surgery.

MEDICINE

In the 1970s, the first MRI (magnetic resonance imagery) and CAT (computed tomography imaging) scan were used. Using these inventions, doctors can see things inside people's bodies without doing surgery. Next, came the use of tiny instruments, medical robots, and lasers (a concentrated beam of light first discovered in the 1950s) to repair damage in very small or delicate body parts. These inventions caused less damage to the patient than traditional surgery.

Another very important effort in the field of medicine is called the Human Genome Project. It is an international collaboration, begun in the mid-1980s, to map the arrangement of chemical codes, called DNA, that are found in the genes of each cell in the human body. Scientists use computers, robotics, and lasers in this very complex work. If the entire chemical code of each cell can be determined and mapped, then scientists may be able to find out about changes in DNA codes that, for example, may cause certain diseases. They may then be able to treat the diseases. Police also use DNA evidence to help solve crimes, because each person has unique DNA.

COMPUTERS AND COMPACT DISCS

Today we use computers everywhere. The first mainframe computers were huge. They took up whole rooms and many people were needed to operate them. Now we have personal computers (PCs) that use a microprocessor, or "chip," a small slice of material that contains electronic parts and connectors to operate the computer. Today, microprocessors are found in everything from appliances to cars. Computers can recognize voices and signatures, and can store billions of pieces of information. Faster chips and newer versions are introduced almost yearly.

Compact disc technology, standardized in 1981, allows users to store very large amounts of information, including music.

A microprocessor is a tiny silicon chip that is the heart of a computer.

SPACE EXPLORATION

Scientists developed the space shuttle, a reusable aircraft in which people can travel into space on a mission and return. In 1986, one of the shuttles, the *Challenger*, exploded after takeoff, and all flights were halted until 1988. Even after a second tragic loss of a space shuttle in 2003, however, shuttles will continue to fly to retrieve and repair satellites and to visit the space station.

Space exploration also uses unmanned satellites, one of which reached the planet Venus in 1989 and still sends back pictures. Others are exploring Mars and beyond.

This experimental car is fueled with a gas pump *and* an electric cord.

TRANSPORTATION

On land, the first high-speed train began to operate in France in 1981, reaching a record speed of 300 mph (482 km) in 1989. Since then, high-speed trains have begun operation in Japan and the United States.

The makers of automobiles continue to experiment with ways to use fuel other than gasoline. Some inventors are trying to build a car powered by solar (sun) energy. There are also a number of hybrid cars (cars that use gasoline and electricity or another type of power) being developed. As of 2004, several companies have built such hybrid cars, but they are more expensive than regular cars.

Inventors have also developed better ways to explore under the sea with submersibles.

In 1985, a U.S. deep-sea craft (a robot submarine with video cameras) called *Argo* discovered the wreck of the *Titanic*, a ship that sank in 1912 when it hit an iceberg, and in 1989 it found the wreck of a German battleship from World War I. In 1993, scientists developed a submersible robot that can go as deep as four miles down in the ocean and stay for as long as a year. These robots can take pictures of the ocean bottom so we can learn more about life there.

COMMUNICATION

In 1988, the first fiber optic cable laid in the Atlantic Ocean, between the United States and Europe, can carry 37,800 voice messages at one time. These messages travel faster and over longer distances than before. In the 1990s, cellular (cell) phones, which *transmit* (send) messages from a signal tower, allow messages to travel without cable or telephone lines.

Cables, or telephone lines, are also being used differently. They are not just for voice calls, but also for sending written material or pictures, even movies and high definition television (HDTV).

We also can know where we are on the Earth to within twenty-five feet by using the Global Positioning System (GPS). With this system, a signal is received from several satellites, and the direction of the signal and distance from the satellite can be computed to locate the point on the Earth from which the signal came. It is available in some automobiles to help drivers find their destinations.

Lasers took on new, non-medical, uses in the 1980s and later. They are used for printers, scanners, underwater photography, and X-rays. They can send vast amounts of information—billions more bits than cable. Another old invention with a new use is radar. In 1988, the National Weather Service used the first Doppler radar system. It detects changes in wind speed and direction to help better forecast changes in the weather.

A GPS satellite orbits the Earth.

UNDERSTANDING WHAT YOU READ | **Finding More Information**

You have just read about recent technological inventions. You may already be using some of them. Select one invention and find out more about it. Use the Internet to find the answers to the following questions:

1. Who was the inventor (or who were the inventors)?

2. How is this technological invention used today? Who uses it?

3. Could this technological invention be used in other ways? Is someone working on this change?

4. Was this technological invention used for something different at first?

Use the information to write a short report. Read your report to the rest of the class and answer their questions. Follow the guidelines in Unit 3 (pages 88–89) to develop and present your report.

Media is the plural of *medium*. A newspaper is a medium, or means of communication. Media refers to all the ways that information and entertainment are communicated to people. Newspapers, magazines, movies, television, radio, and the Internet are often called "the media."

Work with two or three classmates. Discuss the ways that each of you uses the media. Estimate how often each person uses each medium in one week. For example, if you read the newspaper every day, write *7*. If you go to a movie once a week, write *1*. Then add together the information from all the groups to make a class chart like the one below. Complete the chart with the total number of times that the class uses each type of medium in one week. Then write some examples of what types of information people in your class have learned from each medium. For example, how many people learn about today's news from TV or the Internet? About sports from TV or the newspaper? About fashion from magazines or movies?

	NEWSPAPERS	MAGAZINES	MOVIES	TELEVISION	RADIO	THE INTERNET
Number of times used per week						

Information Explosion

TELEVISION, SATELLITES, AND CABLE TV

Since the 1950s, when television was widely introduced, people have been tuned into the "box." It gives Americans an instant look at the world. By the end of the 20th century, television images of events could be seen around the world as they were happening. In the 1990s, when the first Gulf War began, people were watching the evening news broadcast from Baghdad as the bombing began. The development of satellite and cable television has meant that television can reach more people with more channels than ever before. Today, more people are aware of what is happening, as it happens, even half a world away.

THE INTERNET

The rapid growth of the Internet has given people even more information in "real time." The user of the Internet can find out almost any information about anything—people, places, history, weather, and travel for instance. Internet users can also have person-to-person conversations.

TV news vans transmit information with satellite antennas and dishes during the Sniper Killings in Rockville, Maryland, 2002.

HOW OTHERS SEE THE UNITED STATES

The same media that people *inside* the United States use so often has also given people *outside* the United States a view of life in this country. From fashions to music to movies and sports events, people around the world can see what Americans do for a living, what they wear and eat, how they play, and what movies and music are popular. Much of what people who come to this country from other areas of the world know about America and about the English language comes from the media.

TELEVISIONS IN AMERICA		
Year	Number of Households with Televisions	Percentage of American Homes with Televisions
1945	5,000	Less than 0.1
1950	3,880,000	9.0
1955	30,700,000	64.5
1960	45,750,000	87.1
1970	59,550,000	95.2
1980	76,300,000	97.9
2000	100,800,000	98.2

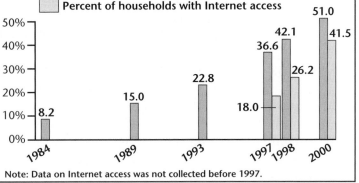

COMPUTERS AND INTERNET ACCESS IN THE HOME: 1984 TO 2000
(Civilian non-institutional population)

- Percent of households with a computer
- Percent of households with Internet access

Note: Data on Internet access was not collected before 1997.

UNDERSTANDING WHAT YOU READ | Evaluating Information Sources

How accurate is media information about real life in the United States? Work in groups of three or four. Your teacher will assign one medium to each group (television, newspapers, magazines, movies, or the Internet). Investigate two samples of the medium assigned to your group to analyze how each describes life in the United States. Discuss the following questions with your group, then write your answers in your notebook. Present your conclusions to the class.

1. Describe the people that appear in this medium. (What do they look like? How are they dressed?)

2. What kinds of jobs do people have? Are they low-, medium-, or high-skilled jobs? How can you tell?

3. Where do people live? What are their houses or apartments like?

4. What kinds of transportation do people in this medium use?

5. What kinds of things do people in this medium do for fun?

After each group has presented its report, discuss the following question as a class: Which medium do you think presents the most accurate information? Why do you think so?

UNDERSTANDING WHAT YOU READ | Using Graphs

1. In your notebook, write a sentence that describes:
   a. the graph about televisions in the United States
   b. the graph about computers in the United States

2. What does the information in the two graphs above tell you about Americans and technology?

Vocabulary

You will need to understand these words as you read about the four men who were U.S. presidents between 1980 and 2003. In your notebook, match each vocabulary word on the left to its definition on the right. Then discuss the meaning of the word with a classmate, and use it in a sentence in your notebook.

1. bankrupt

2. deficit

3. hostage

4. impeach

5. implement

6. income tax

7. platform

8. policies

9. recession

10. science fiction

11. surplus

a. person taken prisoner and held for exchange of money or other advantages

b. rules used by the government or business

c. more than what is needed; opposite of deficit

d. to begin or carry out

e. percentage of salary or profit paid to the government

f. story set in the future that uses new inventions

g. to accuse a public official of a crime

h. debts owed by the government; opposite of surplus

i. without money or credit; unable to pay debts

j. statement of the beliefs or goals of a political party

k. a widespread slowdown in business activity with increased unemployment

Four Recent Presidents

Every U.S. president has had ideas about how to govern. Presidential candidates and their political parties develop a *platform* that outlines their ideas to the voters. Then people vote based on whether they think the candidate's platform is a good one and whether they think the candidate can do what is promised.

Once elected, however, it is often difficult for any president to carry out the platform exactly as promised. Each new president inherits both the problems and the successes of the previous president. For example, if the previous president has implemented a policy that most people like, it is difficult for the next president to go against that policy. Similarly, if the previous president was not successful in solving a problem, or if new problems have arisen, the new president will have to try to find solutions.

As you read about the next four presidents, think about how each one's platform was influenced by the president or presidents before him, and what domestic or foreign decisions were made and carried out.

RONALD REAGAN (1981–1989)

Ronald Reagan was an actor in Hollywood and then the governor of California before being elected president. On the day that he took office as president, the fifty Americans taken hostage in Iran during Carter's presidency were released. People were very happy that these Americans were safe and free after nearly a year as prisoners. Reagan's presidency started off with enthusiasm and good will.

Reagan expressed pride and optimism in the United States. He was often called "the great communicator" because he explained complicated issues in a simple way. His policies included cuts in taxes and increases in military spending to fight the Cold War with the Soviet Union, which he called the "evil empire." He wanted to make sure that the United States could defend itself. To do this, he proposed a missile defense system (Strategic Defense Initiative—SDI) to protect the nation. This project would be extremely expensive, and some people did not think it would work. People against the project thought it sounded more like science fiction than real science, so they called it "Star Wars" after the 1970s science fiction movie of the same name. However, money was allocated to begin the project.

Reagan believed that by cutting income taxes, individuals and companies would have more money to spend. With more money left over, companies would be able to hire more workers and reduce unemployment. This policy became known as "Reaganomics." But a severe recession occurred in the early 1980s and lasted for several years. Because people were paying fewer taxes, there was less money to pay for federal programs, so the government borrowed money. The federal deficit then grew larger and larger.

> "The poverty rate, which fell as low as 11 percent in the 1970s, moved higher in the Reagan years and jumped during the last couple of years. [In 1991], an estimated 36 million people—or about 14.7 percent of the total population—were living in poverty."
>
> —Business Week, *May 18, 1992*

U.S. President Ronald Reagan and Soviet President Mikhail Gorbachev in Red Square, Moscow, November 1985

GEORGE H.W. BUSH (1989–1993)

The next president, George H.W. Bush, had been Ronald Reagan's vice president. He continued with many of Reagan's ideas and policies. Before he was elected, part of Bush's platform was that he would not raise taxes. However, the federal deficit kept growing and by 1992 had reached $290 billion. Bush had to change his plan because the government owed so much money. President Bush was also interested in education. He hosted a meeting of all the state governors and the mayor of the District of Columbia in 1989. This group developed and approved a set of goals designed to improve public schools.

Two major international events happened during Bush's presidency. The first was in 1989, when conversations with the West by Soviet leader Mikhail Gorbachev brought an end to the forty-year-old Cold War. Germans

The fall of the Berlin Wall, November 1989

Oilfield fires in Kuwait during Operation Desert Storm, March 1991

WILLIAM JEFFERSON CLINTON (1993–2001)

Bill Clinton, who had been the governor of Arkansas, was elected president in 1992. President Clinton ran on a platform that focused on improving the economy. He worked to lower government expenses and reduce the federal deficit. By the time he left office in 2001, the government had a surplus of money instead of a deficit.

President Clinton was also interested in laws that would help the environment, children, schools, and health care. He worked on education goals, using federal money to assist in the development of learning standards. The first president in a post–Cold War world, Clinton was also very involved in foreign issues. He assisted in bringing peace to Northern Ireland and a cease-fire in the Balkans. He worked with the leaders of other nations in this process. He also followed the

tore down the Berlin Wall, which had been a physical reminder of the division between communism and democracy. The countries that had been part of the Soviet Union became independent countries. Russia remained the largest of these countries, but without as much power as before. Now, instead of two superpowers in the world, there was only one: the United States.

The second event was the first Gulf War, a war that was fought in the Middle East near the Persian (or Arabian) Gulf. Iraq had invaded its neighboring country, Kuwait. Western nations feared that if Iraq conquered Kuwait, they would no longer be able to buy oil from these two countries. After a UN embargo on Iraq failed to end the Iraqi occupation, a coalition of nations led by the United States attacked Iraq, driving the Iraqi troops out of Kuwait in two months. Following the Gulf War, the United Nations placed an embargo on Iraqi trade and sent in inspectors to check that Iraq was not producing any more weapons.

President Clinton signs the North American Free Trade Agreement aimed at protecting workers and the environment, September 14, 1993

work of President Carter to try to bring a solution to the conflict in the Middle East.

President Clinton's last few years in office were clouded by an investigation into his personal behavior. He was impeached (brought to trial) by the House of Representatives in 1999. If a president is impeached by the House, the Senate then decides if the conduct is so bad that the president should be removed from office. Although the senators did not like the president's behavior, they did not vote to remove him from office.

AN UNUSUAL ELECTION

The presidential election in 2000 was between Al Gore, who had been Clinton's vice president, and George W. Bush, governor of Texas and son of George H.W. Bush. This election was unusual because the election was not decided until almost six weeks after the vote in November. Gore received more votes than Bush, but presidential elections in the United States are not decided by popular vote (the actual number of votes) but by the votes of the Electoral College.

The Electoral College consists of a group of people who represent each state and the District of Columbia. The number of people in the Electoral College depends on each state's number of members of Congress (plus three votes for the District of Columbia). To be elected president, one candidate must receive a majority of the 538 votes.

The Electoral College's vote was delayed because there was a dispute about the popular vote in Florida. Eventually the election was decided by the Supreme Court of the United States. Their decision meant that George W. Bush became president.

GEORGE W. BUSH (2001–)

George W. Bush became president in 2001. His policies were much like those of Reagan and George H.W. Bush. To decrease the federal government's surplus, he proposed a large tax cut that became law in 2001. By 2002, the surplus was gone and the government had a new federal deficit. Many companies became bankrupt and unemployment increased. Then several large corporations were caught cheating—they had said that they were earning money when actually they had huge deficits. Because of these lies, thousands of employees were left without jobs and without pensions for their retirement. Congress and the president began working to pass new laws and enforce current laws to punish the corporations that had cheated.

During his campaign for president, George W. Bush had said that he did not want the United States to become involved in conflicts in other countries and wanted to lower taxes and send federal money back to the states. Once in the presidency, he tried to follow some of these plans, but not others. The years to come will determine how effective his decisions are.

UNDERSTANDING WHAT YOU READ | Study Questions

1. Work with a partner. Reread the sections about each president. Write two questions about each president in your notebook. At least one question should be a *why* question.

2. Now sit in groups of four or five classmates. Take turns asking the people in your group questions. When all the questions have been asked and answered, discuss the questions. Which were easy? Which were difficult? Write the three most difficult questions and their answers in your notebook.

Interpreting Political Cartoons

Political cartoonists draw pictures to tell the reader how they or the people they know feel about someone or some event. You can often tell how they feel by the way they draw the people in the cartoon or what symbols or words they use in their drawing.

Look at the three cartoons. They each tell you something about recent presidents. Work in small groups. Each group should work on one cartoon. Study the cartoon and answer the following questions:

1. Who are the people in the cartoon? How do you know?

2. Describe what is happening in the cartoon.

3. What does this cartoon tell you about this president?

4. Decide on a good title for the cartoon.

Share your answers and titles with the class.

BEFORE YOU READ **Finding Out about Imported Products**

Look at the products you use every day at home and at school. Where were these products made? Work with a classmate and list as many countries of manufacture as possible for each type of product listed below.

- clothes and shoes
- electronics (such as TV, radio, CD player, DVD player)
- sports equipment
- music
- food
- office and classroom supplies

Make a class chart that shows each item and its country of manufacture. Then discuss what you have learned about trade between the United States and other countries.

Globalization

Globalization refers to the increasing interdependence of nations around the world. Events or problems in one country affect not just their own people, but often the governments, people, and economies of other countries. Globalization has increased because of better transportation, faster communication, and increased trade among countries.

In the last twenty years of the 20th century, the United States became much more politically involved in the world outside its borders. The collapse of the Soviet Union, the United States's powerful enemy, meant the United States was the strongest military power in the world. Because most countries considered the United States to be the only "superpower," its role in world affairs became even larger.

The worldwide trade of many U.S. corporations also drives U.S. involvement in other countries. These corporations think globally and try to sell their products around the world. International industries move their factories near the places where they sell the products. For example, U.S. car companies like Ford and General Motors make cars in Europe, South America, and the United States, just as Japanese car companies make cars in the United States and Japan. Trade treaties with Mexico and China have opened up new markets for U.S. goods and also allowed those countries to sell their products in the United States.

The international issues are complex. Leaders in the United States must work with leaders in other countries who often have very different ideas about how to organize their governments and their economies. In many parts of the world, conflicts and wars have caused not only changes in governments but also great damage to a country's environment and suffering for its people. While the United States's most important duty is to protect its own people and its own business interests, it also tries to help other nations when they have economic needs.

UNDERSTANDING WHAT YOU READ **Extending Information**

The United States has become involved in many parts of the world in recent years. What do you now know about each area or country below? Locate each one on a world map. Look for additional information about these areas in the library, newspapers, and on the Internet.

- Afghanistan
- Bosnia
- Ethiopia
- Iran
- Iraq

- Israel
- Kuwait
- Liberia
- Pakistan
- Palestine

- Saudi Arabia
- Somalia
- South Africa
- Sudan

Work with a classmate. Discuss what you have learned in this unit and in your research about each of these areas and its relation to the United States. Write what you know in your notebook. Then share this information with the class.

What learning strategies did you use to write your notes about maps? Write them in your notebook.

LEARNING STRATEGY

Identifying What You Already Know

What is terrorism? What do terrorists do? What reasons do they give for their actions? What should a nation do if ordinary citizens are attacked or killed by terrorists?

Work in groups of three to discuss your ideas about these questions. Report your ideas to the rest of the class. Write what you learned in your notebook.

The Events of September 11, 2001

On September 11, 2001, devastating surprise attacks on the World Trade Center in New York City and on the Pentagon in Washington, DC, changed many things for the United States and the world. Almost 3,000 people, both Americans and citizens from more than eighty other countries, were killed in the attacks. The United States and the world were in shock. The United States responded first by working with its allies to find out who was responsible for the terrorist acts. It was learned that the terrorists were being protected by the Taliban government of Afghanistan, so the United States, with the support of most of the countries of the world, attacked and destroyed that government. But terrorism continues to be a problem worldwide.

THE WAR AGAINST TERRORISM

Since the attacks, the "war against terrorism" has been an ongoing cost for the United States. Income from taxes to the government has decreased as a result of tax cuts and a weak economy, creating a deficit. The two major political parties—Republican and Democrat—hold different views about policies and how to direct federal dollars. While everyone agrees with the need to fight terrorism and to protect American lives, it is very difficult to know how this can be done and what it might mean for individuals. As has been true at other times in the history of the United States, people have different ideas about which problems are most important and how to solve them. Debates involving different points of view in Congress and within the Executive Branch continue to be important for all people in the United States and in the world.

One cartoonist's reaction to the terrorist attack, published on September 12, 2001

WE ARE MAKING HISTORY NOW

Right after the attacks on September 11, 2001, it was difficult for anyone to understand what this might mean for the United States. Not since the attack on Pearl Harbor in 1941 during World War II had the United States suffered an attack with such loss of life, and this time it was against civilians rather than against a military target.

An attack like the one on September 11 influences decisions made by a government and its people. In the United States, the federal government proposed many changes, including a new structure of the U.S. government. For example, a new federal department, the Department of Homeland Security, was created to oversee security within the country. In addition, investigations were begun to try and find out why the attack happened and whether

> *"Now we are in the presence of history in the raw— history that moves one not only to know but to act. This is the history we are making now."*
>
> —*Roger J. Spiller,* Our Chances of a Happier Ending

it could have been prevented. The government also looked at federal laws to decide if any changes needed to be made.

Congress passed the *USA Patriot Act* in October 2001 to give law enforcement greater *latitude* (ability) to pursue suspected terrorists by electronic surveillance (spying) or telephone wire taps. Critics of this Act wonder if its provisions may invade individual privacy. But the answers are not yet known. All sides will continue to observe and decide how best to balance individual rights and the needs of the nation.

INTERPRETING IMAGES Looking Back, Looking Forward

There are threads, the things we have in common, that tie the people and events of U.S. history together over time and across regions. They make this country whole. They weave together ideas of liberty, family, pursuit of happiness, and service to country.

Work with a classmate. Study the pictures on pages 144–145. They illustrate different places, people, and times of our history. Each image also tells a story of the individuals who make up the United States. Discuss the following questions, and write your ideas in your notebook.

1. What stories do the pictures tell you about the people who make up the United States?

2. What do you know about the times and places in which these people lived?

3. What thread or threads does each picture illustrate? Explain your answer.

4. How do the pictures illustrate what the Reverend Jesse Jackson said about America being a quilt?

Add Your Story to the Quilt of U.S. History

Make a class exhibit that shows photographs and other artifacts of each person's family history.

> "America is not like a blanket—one piece of unbroken cloth, the same color, the same texture, the same size. America is more like a quilt—many pieces, many colors, many sizes, all woven and held together by a common thread."
>
> —*Reverend Jesse Jackson*

Four Presidents: 1980–2004

Four presidents served during the last twenty years of the 20th century and the beginning of the 21st century. Three of these presidents had similar ideas about domestic and foreign issues and policies, while one had a different viewpoint on these. The United States was involved in many important events during this period, and these events continue to have an impact on our government and on our lives.

PRESIDENT	EVENTS

1980

Ronald Reagan

1981 – Hostages released by Iran
1982 – Reagan begins financing guerrilla army in Nicaragua (Contras) opposing communist Sandinistas
1983 – U.S. military barracks in Beirut, Lebanon, attacked by terrorists; over 200 U.S. Marines killed
    Reagan proposes Space-Based Defense Initiative (SDI) or "Star Wars"

1985

1986 – Federal deficit to $221 billion
    Space shuttle *Challenger* explodes on takeoff
    Immigration Reform and Control Act grants amnesty to some illegal aliens
1987 – Reagan and Soviet Premier Gorbachev sign treaty to reduce nuclear weapons

George H.W. Bush

1989 – Fall of Berlin Wall
    End of Cold War
    Exxon Valdez oil spill

1990

1991 – First Gulf War
    Collapse of Soviet Union
1992 – Federal deficit reaches $290 billion; national debt over $3 trillion
    Race riots in Los Angeles after videotaped beating of Rodney King
    U.S. intervention in Somalia
1993 – Peace agreement between Israel and Palestinians
    World Trade Center bombed by terrorists

William J. Clinton

1994 – Congress approves NAFTA treaty trade agreement
    United States withdraws from Somalia
    Republicans take control of U.S. House of Representatives
    Apartheid ends in South Africa and Nelson Mandela is elected president

1995 1995 – Bomb destroys government building in Oklahoma City

1996 – Welfare laws revised

1998 – Clinton announces federal budget surplus
    Bosnian peace agreement
1999 – United States returns Panama Canal to Panama
    Clinton impeached

George W. Bush

2001 – Terrorist attacks on New York City and Washington, DC
Tax cut passed
2002 – Defeat of Taliban in Afghanistan in campaign against terrorism
Scandals in large corporations
New European Union currency (the Euro) begins January 1
Campaign finance reform bill passed
2003 – Gulf War II
Columbia space shuttle explodes
Federal deficit climbs to $374 billion; national debt to nearly $7 trillion

---

UNDERSTANDING WHAT YOU READ Using a Time Line

The presidential time line shows some of the events that happened during the terms of U.S. presidents between 1980 and 2003. Some of the events on the time line show information that was not in the unit readings. Some of the events in the readings are not on the time line.

Work with a group of two or three classmates to construct a detailed time line of one of the four presidents that served between 1980 and 2004. Include information from the readings. Look up new information on the presidential time line in reference books or on the Internet so that you understand the event. Use the Internet and newspapers to find out about important events that happened after 2003.

Use your group's detailed time line to list events in two categories: domestic and foreign. Then decide whether the president you studied focused more on domestic policy or more on foreign policy, or about the same on both. Present your conclusions to the class.

Write the Next Unit

Unit 5 ends in 2003. What events that have occurred since that time would you include in a Unit 6?

Work with one or more classmates to discuss the events that you would add. Then discuss what you think might happen next. What important laws might be passed? What decisions about foreign policy might be made? What decisions might be made about domestic policy? Where will you be? What will you do? What will your children do? What will the biggest issues be in the next ten years?

Give reasons for your answers. Share your ideas with the class.

Appendix A

Using Maps

Look at the map below and the map on page 74 to answer questions about the end of World War II. Write your answers in your notebook.

1. When did the Russians save the city of Stalingrad from the German army?
2. How much time was there between the Battle of Anzio and the fall of Berlin?
3. Make a time line of the events on the map.
4. Write a paragraph describing the events on your time line.

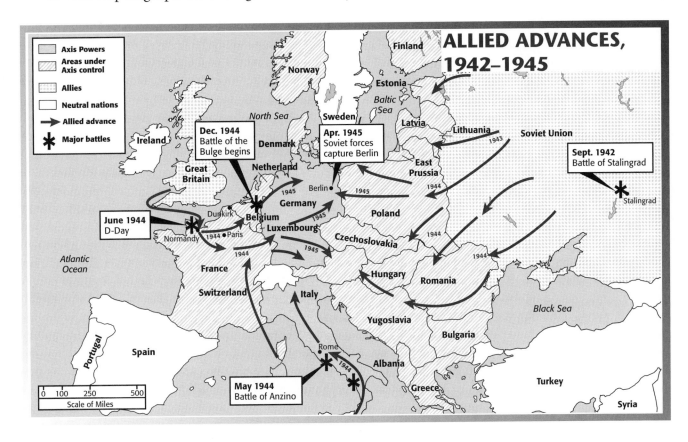

Glossary

a	hat, cap	**j**	jam, enjoy	
ā	age, face	**k**	kind, seek	
ä	father, hot	**l**	land, coal	
		m	me, am	
b	bad, rob			
ch	child, much	**n**	no, in	
d	did, red	**ng**	long, bring	

s	say, yes	**ə** represents:	
sh	she, rush	**a** in about	
t	tell, it	**e** in taken	
th	thin, both	**i** in pencil	
TH	then, smooth	**o** in lemon	
		u in circus	

e	let, best
ē	equal, be
ėr	term, learn

ō	open, go
ȯ	order, all
oi	oil, voice
ou	house, out

u	cup, butter
u̇	full, put
ü	rule, move

f	fat, if
g	go, bag
h	he, how

p	paper, cup
r	run, try

v	very, save
w	will, woman
y	young, yet
z	zero, breeze
zh	measure, seizure

i	it, pin
ī	ice, like

accomplishment (ē·'käm'plish) Something that you achieve or are able to do well.

accord (ə·kord') An agreement.

advantage (əd·van'tij) Something that helps you.

advocate (ad'və·ket') To strongly support a particular way of doing things.

alliance (ə·lī'əns) A close agreement or connection between people or countries.

ally (a'lī) A person or country that helps another (plural: *allies*).

amendment (ə·mend'mənt) A section that is added to a document.

annex (ə'neks) To take control of a country or area next to your own, especially by using force.

appeasement (ə·pēz'mənt) Something done or given to someone to make him/her less angry.

appliance (ə·plī'ens) A piece of electrical equipment, such as a refrigerator or a dishwasher, used in people's homes.

armistice (är'mə·stəs) Agreement to stop fighting.

arrangement (ə·rānj'mənt) A plan or agreement that something will happen.

assassinate (ə·sa'sən·at') To murder a leader.

assemble (ə·sem'blē) To put together.

assembly line An arrangement of machines, equipment, and workers in which work passes from operation to operation in a direct line until the product is complete.

astronaut (as'trə·nȯt') Someone who travels in space.

atomic bomb A very powerful bomb that causes an explosion by splitting atoms.

bankrupt (bang'krəpt) Without money or credit; unable to pay debts.

barbed wire Wire with short sharp points on it, usually used for making fences.

bilingual (bī·ling'gwəl) Able to speak two languages equally well.

bill (bil) A plan for a new law.

blockade (blä·kād') The action of surrounding an area with soldiers or ships to keep people or supplies from leaving or entering a place.

boarding house A private house where you pay to sleep and eat.

bonus (bo'nəs) Money added to someone's pay, especially as a reward for good work.

bootleg (büt·leg) To make and sell products illegally.

budget deficit A situation in which there is not enough money to pay expected expenses.

campaign (kam·pān') A series of actions done to get a result, especially in business or politics.

candidate (kan'də·dat') A person who hopes to be chosen for a job or a political position.

casualty (ka'zhəl·tē) Someone who is hurt in an accident or battle.

cease-fire (sēs fīr) An agreement for both sides in a war to stop fighting for a period of time.

censure (sen'shər) To officially criticize someone for something he or she has done wrong.

chancellor (chan'sə·lər) The head of the government in some countries.

civil rights (si'vəl rīts) The legal rights that every individual in a particular country has, such as the right to have the same treatment whatever one's race or religion.

civilian (sə·vil'yən) A person who is not in the military.

coalition (ko'ə·li'shən) A union of separate political parties or people who join together for a special purpose, usually for a short time.

communications (kə·myü'nə·kā'shənz) The various ways of sending and receiving information, such as radio, telephone, television.

communism (käm'yə·ni'zəm) A political system in which the government controls all the production of food and goods and in which there is no privately owned property.

concentration camp A heavily armed prison for political prisoners or for people who are considered dangerous during a war.

condition (kən·di'shən) The state of someone or something.

confront (kən·fr'shən) To try to make someone admit he or she has done something wrong.

confrontation (kän'frən·tā'shən) A situation where there is a lot of angry disagreement.

conquer (käng'kər) To win control of a land or country by force.

consequence (kän'sə·kwens') Something that happens as the result of something else.

conservation (kän'sə·vā'shən) The protection of natural things, such as wild animals, forests, or beaches, from being harmed or destroyed.

containment (kən·tān'mənt) The act of keeping something controlled, such as the power of an unfriendly country.

contaminate (kən·ta'mə·nāt') To spoil something by adding a dangerous or poisonous substance to it.

corral (kə·ral') An enclosed area where animals such as cattle and horses are kept.

corruption (kə·rəp'shən) Dishonest or immoral behavior.

crisis (krī'səs) A very bad or dangerous situation.

culture (kəl'chər) The beliefs, customs, and way of life of a particular society.

custodial work A job that involves taking care of a building.

custom (kəs'təm) Something that is done by people in a particular society because it is traditional.

czar (zär) The ruler in Russia before 1917.

deficit (de'fə·sət) The difference between the amount of money that a company or country has and the higher amount that it needs.

delegate (de'li·gət) A person chosen by vote to go to a meeting and represent voters.

democracy (di·mä'krə·sē') A form of government in which the people rule, either by voting directly or by electing representatives.

desegregate (d ē·se'gri·gāt') To end a system in which people of different races are kept separate.

destruction (di·strək'shən) The act or process of destroying something.

depression (di·pre'shən) A long period when businesses are not very active and many people do not have jobs.

détente (dā·tänt') A relaxing of international tensions.

dictator (dik'tā'tər) A strong leader who is not fair and often uses soldiers to control people.

discrimination (dis·kri'mə·nā'shən) Unfair treatment of some people because of the color of their skin, where they come from, or other factors.

dispose (di·spoz') To get rid of something.

DNA (dē·en·ā) Deoxyribonucleic acid: an acid that carries genetic information in a cell.

doctrine (däk'trən) A belief or set of beliefs, especially religious or political beliefs.

domestic (də·mes'tik) Happening within one's country or one's home.

double (də'bəl) To become twice as large.

draft (draft) 1. to make mechanical drawings 2. to select a person for military service

drought (drout) A long period of dry weather when there is not enough water.

election (i·lek'shən) A time when you vote to choose someone for an official position.

embargo (im·bär'go') An official order to stop trade with another country.

emissions (ē·mi'shənz) Gases, smoke, etc., that are sent out into the air from cars, factories, etc.

endangered (in·dān'jərd) Soon might not exist.

environment (in·vī'rə(n)·mənt) The land, water, and air in which people, animals, and plants live.

equality (i·kwä'lə·tē) Having the same opportunities and rights.

ethnic (eth'nik) Relating to a particular race, nation, tribe, or culture.

exile (eg'zīl) A situation in which someone is forced to leave his or her country and live in another country, usually for political reasons.

fascism (fa'shi'zəm) An extreme political system in which people's lives are completely controlled by the state.

fast-food restaurant A restaurant that prepares and serves food quickly and cheaply.

federal (fe'də·rəl) Relating to the central government of a country that controls a group of states.

fire on To shoot at.

foreign policy (fôr'ən pä'lə·sē) The policy of one country toward other countries.

fortune (fôr'chən) A large amount of money.

fragile (fra'jəl) Easily broken or damaged.

gangster (gang'stər) A member of a group of violent criminals.

garment (gär'mənt) A piece of clothing, such as a shirt or a dress.

genocide (je'nə·sīd') The deliberate murder of a national or racial group.

global warming An increase in the world's temperature, caused by an increase of carbon dioxide around the Earth.

globalization (glo'bə·lə·zā'shən) Interdependence of nations around the world in terms of trade, etc.

goods (gùdz) Things that are produced in order to be sold.

government (gə'vər(n)·mənt) The group of people or the system that controls or rules a state, country, or local area.

heritage (her'ə·tij) The traditional beliefs, values, customs, etc., of a family or country.

high-skilled job A position that requires college or technical training, such as a doctor, a lawyer, a teacher.

high-tech industry Companies that use a high level of technology, such as computer companies.

hostage (häs'tij) A prisoner who is held until a condition is met, such as payment of money, promise to stop fighting, admission of fault.

huge (hyüj) Enormous; very large.

illegal (il·lē'gəl) Not allowed by law.

immigrant (i'mi·grənt) A person who comes into a new country to settle and live.

impeach (im·pēch') To accuse a public official of a crime.

implement (im'plə·mənt) To begin or carry out.

income tax (in'kəm taks) Percentage of salary or profit paid to the government.

industry (in'dəs·trē) A business that produces and sells things.

inflation (in·flā'shən) When prices of goods and services rise too high.

inhumane (in'hyü·mān') Treating people or animals in a cruel and unacceptable way.

injured (in'jərd) Hurt or wounded.

insurance (in·shür'əns) A contract that pays for things such as for medical help, auto or home damage or repair.

integrate (in'tə·grāt') To end the practice of separating people of different races in a place or institution such as a school.

integration (in'tə·grā'shən) Combination of people of different ethnicities, languages, etc.

interchangeable part A piece of one machine that can be used in place of the matching piece of another machine.

interest rate The percentage charged by banks as a fee when they lend money; percentage earned by individuals on money saved in a bank.

intern (in'tərn') To put in prison, especially for political reasons.

internment (in·tərn'mənt) Imprisonment, especially for political reasons.

interstate (in'tər·stāt') Between or involving different states.

intolerance (in·täl'rəns) An unwillingness to accept the ways of thinking and behaving that are different from your own.

invade (in·vād') To enter an area using military force.

invention (in·ven'shən) Something completely new that is made for the first time.

investigation (in·ves'tə·gā'shən) A search for information about something by looking or asking questions.

investment (in·ves(t)'mənt) Something that you buy or do because it will be more valuable or useful later.

investor (in·vest'ər) Someone who gives money to a company or bank in order to get a profit later.

irrigation system Man-made system that supplies land with water.

isolate (ī'sə·lāt') To make or keep one person or thing away from other people or things.

jazz (jaz) A type of music with a strong rhythm (improvisation); first played in the United States.

journalist (jər'nəl·ist) A reporter or writer for a newspaper or magazine.

labor (lā'bər) Work, often involving a lot of physical or mental effort.

labor union An organization that represents workers in a particular job.

lay off (lā äf) The act of stopping someone's employment because there is not enough work.

legislators (le'jəs·lā'tòrz) People who make laws.

loan (lon) The amount of money that you borrow from a bank.

lone (lon) Solitary.

low-skilled job A job that requires basic training, such as factory or restaurant work.

lynch (linch) To illegally hang someone; often done by a crowd or mob.

manufactured products Things made in factories.

march (märch) To walk somewhere in a large group to protest about something.

mass production The manufacture of goods in large quantities.

media (mē'dē·ə) A means of mass communication, such as television, radio, newspapers, and the Internet.

migrant worker A person who moves from one place in a country to work in another place in that country.

mineral (min'rəl) A natural substance like iron, coal, or salt that is found in the ground.

minority (mə·nòr'ə·tē) A group of people with different religion, ideas, or ethnicity than the majority of people in a country.

missile (mi'səl) A weapon that can fly over a long distance and explode when it hits something.

monopoly (mə·nä'pə·le) The control of all or most of a business activity.

mutate (mü'tāt') To become different from others of the same kind because of a change in genes.

natural resources Raw materials provided by nature, such as forests, minerals, water supplies.

navy (nā'vē) The ships of a country used for defense or fighting war, and the people of these ships.

negotiate (ni·go'shē·āt') To discuss something in order to reach an agreement.

neighborhood (nā'bər·hùd') A small area of a town, or the people who live there.

neutrality (nü·tra'lə·tē) Staying out of a war.

nuclear (nü'klē·ər) Power that comes from splitting atoms, used for making electricity and the explosive part of some bombs.

nuclear plant A place where nuclear power is produced.

nuclear waste The dangerous materials left over after making nuclear power.

opportunity (ä'pər·tü'nə·tē) A chance or time to do something.

optimistic (äp'tə·mis'tik) Feeling good about your life and the future.

overthrow (o'vər·thro) To get rid of by force.

ozone layer (o'zon') A layer of gases which protects the Earth from the bad effects of the sun.

pest (pest) A small animal or insect that destroys crops or food.

pesticide (pes'ti·sīd') Chemicals that kill insects.

philanthropist (fə·lan'thrə·pist) Someone who gives a lot of money and help to others.

phonograph (fo'nə·graf') Old-fashioned record player.

plantation (plan·tā'shən) A large farm where just one crop is grown, such as cotton, rice, or sugar cane.

platform (plat'fòrm') The statement of beliefs or goals of a political party.

policy (pä'lə·sē) Rules used by the government or business.

pollution (pə·lü'shən) The process of making air, water, or soil dangerously dirty.

population (pä'pyə·lā'shən) The number of people living in a place.

poverty (pä'vər·tē) The opposite of wealth.

prairie (prer'ē) A large open area of land that is covered in wheat or long grass.

preach (prēch) To give a speech about a religious subject, usually in a church.

prejudice (pre'jə·dəs) An unfair opinion about someone that is not based on facts or reason.

pride (prīd) The feeling of pleasure and satisfaction that you have because of something good that you have done.

product (prä'dəkt) Something grown or made and sold.

progressives (prə·gre'sivz) People or groups that work to improve the lives of others.

prohibit (pro·hi'bət) To not allow something by law or force.

property (prä'pər·tē) Something that someone owns.

protest (pro'test) 1. (v) To say or do something publicly to show that you disagree with something or think it is unfair; 2. (n) A strong public complaint, for example a march or a sit-in.

quota (kwo'tə) A particular amount that you are expected to have, or the limit on the amount of something you are allowed to have.

race (rās) A division of humans by certain characteristics, such as shape, skin color, size.

racism (rā'si·zəm) The unfair treatment of people because of their race.

radar (rā'där') A way of finding the position and speed of ships and planes by using radio waves.

radioactivity (rā'dē·o'ak·ti'və·tē) A quality that some substances have that makes them send out radiation.

recession (rē·se'shən) A widespread slowdown in business activity with increased unemployment.

reformer (ri·fòr'mər) Someone who works hard to make a lot of changes in order to improve a government or society.

religious freedom Freedom to follow any religion one chooses.

renaissance (re'nə·säns') Renewal of interest in art and learning in a certain time in history.

reservation (re'zər·vā'shən) An area of land, established by the U.S. government, on which some Native Americans live.

revolution (re'və·lü'shən) A war that is fought to overthrow the ruling government or to change an established system.

riot (rī'ət) A violent fight by an angry crowd of people.

rural areas The farms, not the cities.

salary (sal'rē) Money that you receive as payment for a job.

savanna (sə·va'nə) A plain or grassland with few or no trees.

science fiction Story set in the future that uses new inventions.

segregation (se'gri·g ā'shən) The separation of one group of people from others because of certain characteristics, such as race or religion.

senate (se'nət) One of the groups in a government that make the laws; one of the houses of the U.S. Congress.

settler (set'lər) Someone who goes to live in a new place, often where there were few people before.

shack (shak) A small building that has not been built very well.

share (shar) One of the equal parts into which the ownership of a company is divided.

shelter (shel'tər) A place that protects you from bad weather or danger, or the protection that is given to you.

sit-in (sit'in') A peaceful kind of protest in which a group of people joins together to try to change an unfair situation.

smuggle (smə'gəl) To take something secretly and illegally from one place to another, especially into another country.

social reformer Someone who works to change unfair laws and practices.

sonar (so·när) A method of finding objects by means of sound waves sent out and reflected off the objects.

space shuttle A type of vehicle that can carry people into space and then return to the Earth to be used again.

speakeasy (spēk'ēz'ē) A place where alcohol is illegally sold.

speculation (spe'kyə·lā'shən) The act of buying goods or property, hoping to make a large profit when you sell them.

steel (stē(ə)l) A strong hard metal made from iron, used for things such as knives, machines, or buildings.

stock broker (stäk bro'kər) Someone whose job is to buy and sell shares.

stock market (stäk mär'kət) The place where stocks and shares are sold and bought.

strategic arms Military equipment that a country keeps in case of war.

submarine (səb'mə·rēn') An undersea boat or ship.

surplus (sər'pləs') More than what is needed; opposite of deficit.

surrender (sə·ren'dər) To say that you want to stop fighting because you know that you cannot win.

survive (sər·vīv') Live on; continue alive.

switchboard operator A worker for the telephone company who connects the telephone calls.

tank (tangk) A heavy military vehicle with guns on it, used in land battles.

tap telephones To secretly listen in on the phone conversations of others.

tenement (te'nə·mənt) A large building divided into apartments, especially in a poor area of a city.

territory (te'rə·tor'ē) An area of land owned by a person or country.

textile (teks'tīl') Any material that is made by weaving.

threat (thret) A statement or warning that you will cause someone trouble, pain, or sadness.

torture (tòr'chər) Mental or physical suffering.

treaty (trē'tē) A formal written agreement between two or more countries.

trench (trench) An excavation or hole dug in the ground.

trolley car An electric streetcar that runs on tracks.

troops (trüps) Army or group of soldiers.

U-boat (yü'bot') German submarine.

unconstitutional (ən'kän'stə·tü'shnəl) Not allowed by the rules that govern a country or organization.

unemployed (ən'im·ploid') Without a job.

unemployment (ən'im·ploi'mənt) When people do not have jobs.

unmanned (ən'mand') Not carrying people.

urban areas The cities, not the farms.

veteran (ve'tə·rən) Someone who had been a soldier.

vocational (vo'kā'shə·nəl) Related to an occupation such as secretary or mechanic.

volunteer (vä'lən·tir') Someone who offers to do something without being paid.

vote (vot) To mark a piece of paper, raise your hand, or mark a computer screen to show who you want to elect or which plan you support.

voting bloc A large group of people who share the same political beliefs and will vote the same way.

wages (wā'jəz) Money you get from working at a job.

wealthy (wel'thē) Rich.

withdraw (with·drò') Stop participating.

world power A strong country that is a leader in the world.

wound (wünd) Injury.

yacht (yät) Large, expensive boat.

Websites

The following sites are suggested as valuable sites for further research on the topics in *Land, People, Nation*. All of the sites chosen are from the upper-level domains of government (gov), education (edu), or organization (org), as these sites are more likely to remain active and be regularly updated. If a URL below does not get you to the Web site, type some key words from the reading selection into your Internet search engine to find some other educational Web sites.

AMDOCS—Documents for the Study of American History
http://history.cc.ukans.edu/carrie/docs/amdocs_index.html
This site contains lists of documents on U.S. history that are available on the Web. The documents range from the 15th through the 20th centuries. Documents can be downloaded. The site is clearly indexed and easy to use.

American Memory: Learning Page
http://rs6.loc.gov/ammem/ndlpedu/features/timeline/index.html
This site within the Library of Congress's American Memory collection provides a time line of U.S. history. It includes an easy-to-follow structure that allows the teacher to highlight an era within U.S. history and find topics relevant to that time. The large number of documents, photographs, and maps provide additional materials for teachers and/or students.

National Archives, Washington, DC
http://www.nara.gov
This site provides an introduction to the official documents of the U.S. government (executive, legislative, and judicial branches and all of their departments) held by the National Archives. It includes the 100 milestone documents of U.S. history, including the Declaration of Independence, the Constitution, and the Bill of Rights. Images of the documents and transcripts of their contents may be downloaded from this site. The National Archives Digital Classroom (http://www.nara.gov/education/classrm.html) provides reproducible documents from the National Archives along with teaching methods. A reproducible worksheet that students may use to analyze photographs can also be found at:
http://www.archives.gov/digital_classroom/lessons/analysis_worksheet

History Matters
http://historymatters.gmu.edu
This site is designed for teachers of U.S. history survey courses. It provides an excellent starting point for exploring U.S. history on the Web. It serves as a gateway to online resources and offers unique teaching materials, such as first-person primary documents and threaded discussions on teaching U.S. history.

Corporation for Public Broadcasting
http://www.pbs.org/history/
All of the materials produced by the public broadcasting system are listed on this site. There is a "For Educators" link; links are set for featured sites that change as new programs are developed. The "History" section may be searched by topic. Videos and materials for classroom use are connected to each topic.

National Council for the Social Studies
http://www.ncss.org
This is the site of the professional association of social studies teachers. It has several features of special interest to U.S. history teachers.

Organization of American Historians
http://www.indiana.edu/~oah
The Organization of American Historians, the professional organization for U.S. historians, serves pre-collegiate history teachers through a link on their Web site to "History Teaching Units." This section introduces lesson plans for grades 6–12 based on primary documents.

Standards and Learning Strategies

Unit	Historical Thinking Standards	Learning Strategies	History and Geography Standards
1 **Industrialization and Change: 1865–1900**	• Chronological thinking • Historical research and interpretation • Historical issues analysis • Historical comprehension	**Introduced** Using Imagery, Summarizing, Graphic Organizers, Predicting, Use What You Know, Making Inferences, Selective Attention, Taking Notes, Cooperation, Using Resources *Reminder* Graphic Organizers, Use What You Know, Cooperation, Summarizing, Selective Attention	**History** Era 6. S.1. How rise of corporations, heavy industry, and mechanized farming transformed American people S.2. How new social patterns, conflicts, ideas about the U.S. developed amid massive immigration after 1870 S.3. How Americans grappled with social, economic, and political issues S.4. U.S. policy toward Native Americans after Civil War Era 7. S.1. How Progressives and others addressed problems of industrialization and urbanization **Geography** S.4. Spatial organization of people, places, and environments on the Earth's surface S.6. Understand human and physical characteristics of places and regions
2 **Starting a New Century: 1900–1940**	• Chronological thinking • Historical comprehension • Historical analysis and interpretation • Historical research and issues analysis	**Introduced** Classification *Reminder* Using Imagery, Making Inferences, Use What You Know, Cooperation, Graphic Organizers, Summarizing, Selective Attention, Taking Notes, Predicting, Using Resources	**History** Era 7. S.2. The changing role of the United States in world affairs through World War I S.3. How the United States changed from the end of World War I to 1930, economically, socially, and politically Era 8. S.1, S.2. The causes of the Great Depression and the New Deal and their affects on American society **Geography** S.1. How to use maps and other geographic representations … to acquire, process, and report information from spatial perspective S.6. Human and physical characteristics of places and regions
3 **The United States Becomes a World Leader: 1940–1960**	• Chronological thinking • Historical comprehension • Historical analysis and interpretation • Historical research	*Reminder* Use What You Know, Summarizing, Using Imagery, Selective Attention, Taking Notes, Making Inferences, Predicting, Using Resources, Cooperation	**History** Era 8. S.3. Causes and course of World War II, the war at home and abroad, its reshaping of the U.S. role in the world Era 9. S.1. Economic boom and social change in postwar United States S.1. Understand role of science and technology in a changing society S.2. How Cold War and conflict in Korea influenced domestic and foreign policy S.3. Domestic policies after World War II such as containment and McCarthyism

Unit	Historical Thinking Standards	Learning Strategies	History and Geography Standards
			Geography S.5. Answer geographic questions and communicate the answers in a number of ways to build historic knowledge
4 **Eras of Protest: 1960–1980**	• Chronological thinking • Historical comprehension • Historical analysis, interpretation, and research • Historical issues analysis and decision making	*Reminder* Predicting, Graphic Organizers, Use What You Know, Classification, Summarizing, Selective Attention, Using Resources, Cooperation	**History** Era 9. S.2. Understand how Cold War conflicts in Vietnam influenced domestic and foreign policy S.3. Understand domestic policies such as New Frontier and Great Society, Space Race S.4. Understand issues in the struggle for racial and gender equality and extension of civil liberties Era 10. Understand foreign and domestic policy from Kennedy to Carter S.2. Recognize economic, social, and cultural/technological developments since 1968 **Geography** S.2. Use maps to process information and answer geographic questions
5 **The American Identity: 1980 to the Present**	• Chronological thinking • Historical comprehension • Historical analysis and interpretation • Historical research capabilities • Historical issues analysis and decision making	*Reminder* Cooperation, Taking Notes, Classification, Use What You Know, Making Inferences, Using Resources, Cooperation, Graphic Organizers, Taking Notes, Summarizing, Selective Attention	**History** Era 10. S.1. Understand recent developments in foreign and domestic policy S.2. Recognize economic, social, and cultural developments in contemporary United States **Geography** S.2. Use maps to process information and answer geographic and historical questions

Credits

(DAVA Still Media Depository) (bottom); **p. 67**, Hulton Deutsch Collection/CORBIS (top); Getty Images, Inc. (bottom); **p. 68**, Getty Images, Inc. (top R, bottom L, bottom R); Hulton Deutsch Collection/CORBIS (top L); **p. 70**, Collection of The Norman Rockwell Museum at Stockbridge, Norman Rockwell Art Collection Trust. Printed by permission of the Norman Rockwell Family Agency, © 2004, the Norman Rockwell Family Entities; **p. 71**, National Archives and Records Administration (L); Getty Images, Inc. (R); **p. 72**, Getty Images, Inc. (top L, top C, center L); The Mariner's Museum/CORBIS (center C); Library of Congress (top R, bottom L); National Archives and Records Administration (bottom R, bottom C); **p. 73**, Library of Congress (bottom R, top L); National Archives and Records Administration (top R, center R); Abram Games, Imperial War Museum, London/Dorling Kindersley (center R); **p. 75**, Hulton Deutsch Collection/CORBIS; **p. 76**, U.S. Army, National Archives and Records Administration; **p. 77**, AP/Wide World Photos (top L); Bettmann/CORBIS (bottom R); **p. 79**, Collection of The New-York Historical Society; **p. 80**, Catherine DeVoe; **p. 82**, Getty Images, Inc.; **p. 83**, Library of Congress; **p. 84**, Getty Images, Inc. (top, center); Sunset Boulevard/CORBIS Sygma (bottom); **p. 85**, Tom McHugh/Photo Researchers; **p. 86**, Collection of The Norman Rockwell Museum at Stockbridge, Norman Rockwell Art Collection Trust. Printed by permission of the Norman Rockwell Family Agency, © 2004, the Norman Rockwell Family Entities (top R); Getty Images, Inc. (bottom C); **p. 87**, Charles R. Drew papers, Moorland-Spingarn Research Center, Howard University (center R); Center for Disease Control and Prevention (center C); National Library of Medicine (top R); Los Alamos National Library (top L); Bettmann/CORBIS (center L, bottom R); Unisys Corporation (top C); **p. 90**, Library of Congress (all); **p. 91**, Courtesy of the Anderson, Seid-Beck, Steeves, Winters, Uhl families.

Unit 4

p. 92, Library of Congress (both); **p. 93**, Library of Congress (all); **p. 95**, Bettmann/CORBIS; **p. 97**, U.S. Air Force/National Archives and Records Administration (DAVA Still Media Depository) (top L); National Aeronautics and Space Administration (bottom L, bottom R); **p. 98**, Peace Corps (both); **p. 100**, AP/Wide World Photos (all); **p. 101**, AP/Wide World Photos; **p. 104**, Hulton Deutsch Collection/CORBIS (top L); A. Ramey/PhotoEdit (bottom R); **p. 105**, National Archives and Records Administration; **p. 106**, Bettmann/CORBIS; **p. 108**, Bettmann/CORBIS (both); **p. 111**, AP/Wide World Photos (top L); News Service Photographs. May 4 Collection, Kent State University Libraries and Media Services. Department of Special Collections and Archives (bottom R); **p. 112**, Catherine Ursillo/Photo Researchers; **p. 113**, Woodfin Camp & Associates; **p. 114**, Getty Images, Inc. (bottom L); Bettmann/CORBIS (bottom R); Library of Congress (top R); **p. 115**, Getty Images, Inc. (center C, top R); AP/Wide World Photos (center L, bottom C); Library of Congress (center R); Bettmann/CORBIS (bottom R); The Denver Post (bottom L); **p. 118**, AP/Wide World Photos; **p. 119**, National Archives and Records Administration; **p. 120**, Library of Congress (both); **p. 121**, Getty Images, Inc. (L); Library of Congress (R).

Unit 5

p. 122, National Aeronautics and Space Administration (both); **p. 123**, AP/Wide World Photos (top L, center L, bottom L, top R); Vanessa Vick/Photo Researchers (center R); © Johnny Johnson/Animals Animals (bottom R); **p. 125**, Washington Metropolitan Area Transit Authority; **p. 126**, Library of Congress (top L); Will Hart/PhotoEdit (center L); Getty Images, Inc. (bottom); **p. 128**, Reuters NewMedia Inc./CORBIS; **p. 129**, New Jersey Department of Environmental Protection, a Division of Watershed Management, Artist: Erin Broder (top); AP/Wide World Photos (bottom); **p. 131**, © Yoav Levy/Phototake; **p. 132**, General Electric Corporate Research and Development (center R); Micron Technology (bottom L); **p. 133**, U.S. Department of Defense, Visual Information Center; **p. 134**, Tom Carter/PhotoEdit; **p. 137**, Ronald Reagan Presidential Library; **p. 138**, CORBIS (top L); U.S. Army/National Archives and Records Administration (top R); Reuters/CORBIS (bottom R); **p. 140**, Steve Greenberg, ©1987, Seattle Post-Intelligencer (bottom L); from Herblock: A Cartoonist's Life, Times Books, 1998 (top R); Ed Stein, reprinted with permission of Rocky Mountain News (bottom R); **p. 142**, The Washington Post (top L); Danziger/LA Times Syndicate (bottom R); **pp. 144–145**, Courtesy of the Alvarado, Anderson, Captain, Cheek, Lara, Matsumoto, Seid-Beck, Winters, and Uhl families.

The authors wish to thank the following for their assistance in the preparation of this book: Sue Arya, Jules Canter, Jeffrey McCarthy, James McGrath Morris; Johanna Phillips, and Erin Webreck.

Index

working conditions in, **8, 20, 21, 35**
Fair Labor Standards Act (FLSA), **55**
Farm Security Administration (FSA), **54**
fascism, **65**
Federal Bureau of Investigation (FBI), **119**
federal deficit, **137–139**
Federal Deposit Insurance Corporation (FDIC), **55**
Federal Emergency Relief Administration (FERA), **55**
Federal Housing Act (FHA), **55**
Ford, Gerald, **119, 121**
Ford, Henry, **33**
foreign policy, **118**
Fourteenth Amendment, **105**
France
  in Vietnam, **111**
  in World War I, **41, 44, 45**
  in World War II, **67, 68**
Franco, Francisco, **65**
Friedan, Betty, **106, 115**

Garfield, James A., **28**
Germany
  division of, **77, 138**
  following World War I, **64, 65**
  rise of Hitler in, **65**
  in World War I, **41, 42, 44, 45**
  in World War II, **67–69, 71, 74, 76, 77**
Geronimo, **14**
GI Bill of Rights, **79**
Gilded Age, **5**
Global Positioning System (GPS), **133**
global warming, **130**
globalization, **141**
Gonzalez, Rodolfo, **115**
Gorbachev, Mikhail, **137**
Gore, Al, **130, 139**
Grant, Ulysses S., **4–5, 28**
Grassland Regions, **10**
Great Britain
  in World War I, **41, 42, 44, 45**
  in World War II, **67, 68, 70**
Great Depression, **52–54**
Great Migration, **37**
Great Plains, **10, 11, 14, 23**
Gulf War, **134, 138**
Guthrie, Woody, **114**

Harding, Warren G., **60**
Harlem Renaissance, **49**

Harrison, Benjamin, **28**
Hawaii, annexation of, **4**
Hayakawa, S. I., **115**
Hayes, Rutherford B., **28**
Henderson, Fletcher, **49**
high-tech industries, **124**
highway system, **85**
Hispanic Americans, **105–106**
Hitler, Adolf, **65, 67, 76**
Ho Chi Minh, **82, 111**
Holocaust, **77**
Hoover, Herbert, **53, 54, 60**
Hopi, **13, 16**
Hopper, Grace Murray, **87**
Huerta, Delores, **115**
Hughes, Langston, **49, 59**
Hull House, **21**
Human Genome Project, **132**
Hurston, Zora Neale, **49**

immigrants
  from Asia, **23, 36, 47, 104–105**
  employment for, **23–24, 34, 36, 124–125**
  English language programs for, **24, 104–105**
  from Mexico, **36, 47, 94**
  restrictive laws affecting, **47**
impeachment, **139**
Indian Territory, **13**
Industrial Revolution
  change brought by, **8–9**
  explanation of, **2, 6**
  oil industry during, **7**
  railroads during, **6, 7**
  steel industry during, **7**
  textile industry during, **6, 20**
industry, **6, 7, 20, 86, 124.** *See also* factories
integration, **80**
International Ladies' Garment Workers' Union (ILGWU), **35**
Internet, **134, 135**
internment camps, **73, 94, 104**
inventions
  nineteenth-century, **9, 18–19**
  twentieth-century, **87, 131–133**
Iran, **119, 137**
Iraq, **138**
Israel, **118, 119**
Italy
  fascism in, **65**
  in World War I, **41**

in World War II, **67, 68, 71**

Japan
  immigrants from, **23, 36**
  invasion of China by, **67**
  seizure of Manchuria by, **66**
  in World War II, **68, 71, 74, 76**
Japanese Americans, **73, 80, 94, 104**
Jazz Age, **49**
Jews, **65, 77**
Johnson, Andrew, **4, 28**
Johnson, Lyndon B., **108, 109, 111, 120**

Kennedy, John F., **86, 94, 97, 98, 108, 120**
King, Martin Luther, Jr., **100, 101**
Korea, **82, 104**
Korean War, **82**
Ku Klux Klan (KKK), **47**
Kuwait, **138**

La Causa, **105**
La Raza Unida, **106**
labor unions, **8, 35, 105**
Latin America, **33**
Lau v. Nichols, **105**
laws
  child labor, **21**
  civil rights, **86, 101, 109**
  environmental, **113**
  Progressive era, **39**
League of Nations, **45**
Lend-Lease, **70**
Lenin, V. I., **64, 83**
Lincoln, Abraham, **4**
Lindbergh, Charles, **48**
Lowell, Francis Cabot, **20**
Lowell Girls, **20**
Lusitania, **42**
lynching, **46–47**

Malcolm X, **101**
Marshall, George C., **77**
Marshall Plan, **77**
Marshall, Thurgood, **85**
mass production, **33–34, 52**
McCarthy, Joseph, **83**
McKinley, William, **28, 32, 60**
medicine, **131–132**
Mexican Americans, **36, 47, 94, 105, 106**
Middle East, **118, 119, 138**
migration, **37, 47, 124–125**
monopolies, **8**
Morgan, J. Pierpont, **5**
Morton, "Jelly Roll," **49**

music, **49, 114**
Mussolini, Benito, **65, 67**

National Aeronautics and Space Administration (NASA), **97**
National Association for the Advancement of Colored People (NAACP), **47**
National Farm Workers Association (NFWA), **105**
National Housing Act (NHA), **55**
National Labor Relations Act (NLRA), **55**
National Organization for Women (NOW), **106**
National Youth Administration (NYA), **55**
Native Americans
  equality for, **103–104**
  origin of, **23, 25**
  poverty among, **94**
  on reservations, **14, 94**
  treaties with, **13–14, 103**
Navajo, **13, 16, 75**
Nazis, **65, 77**
Netherlands, **67**
New Deal, **54–55**
Nineteenth Amendment, **47**
Nixon, Richard, **83, 111, 118–121**
North Korea, **82**
North Vietnam, **82**
nuclear arms limitation treaties, **118, 119**

occupations, **124**
oil industry, **7**
Oppenheimer, J. Robert, **87**
Oregon Territory, **13**
Oswald, Lee Harvey, **108**

Paige, Satchel, **48, 49**
Parks, Rosa, **86, 115**
Peace Corps, **98**
Pearl Harbor, **71, 143**
Pei, I. M., **25**
Philippines, **33**
piece work, **34**
Poland, **67**
pollution, **113, 129, 130**
poverty, **21, 94, 109**
prejudice, **80**
presidential platforms, **136**
Progressive movement, **33, 38–39**
Progressives, **38**
Prohibition, **49**
Puerto Rico, **33**

railroads, **6, 7, 11, 132**
Reagan, Ronald, **137, 146**

Reaganomics, **137**
Red Scare, **46**
reformers, **21, 33**
reservations, **13–14, 103**
revolution, **6**
Rickover, Hyman, **87**
Riis, Jacob, **21, 39**
Roaring Twenties, **49**
Rockefeller, John D., **5**
Rockwell, Norman, **70, 86**
Roosevelt, Franklin Delano
 New Deal and, **54–55, 61**
 World War II and, **67,
  70, 71, 81, 90**
Roosevelt, Theodore, **32–33,
 54, 60**
Ruby, Jack, **108**
rural areas, **37, 39, 47**
Rural Electrification
 Administration (REA), **54**
Russia. *See also* Soviet Union
 after collapse of Soviet
  Union, **138**
 purchase of Alaska from,
  4, 32
 in World War I, **41, 42, 44**
Russian Revolution, **42, 64,
 65**
Ruth, Babe, **48, 49**

Sabin, Albert, **87**
Sadat, Anwar, **119**
Salk, Jonas, **87**
SALT I (Strategic Arms
 Limitation Talks), **118**
SALT II (Strategic Arms
 Limitation Talks), **119**
Sauk, **13**
schools
 bilingual and ESL classes
  in, **24, 105**
 changing requirements
  for, **126**
 desegregation of, **85, 86,
  94, 99**
Sears, Roebuck, **34**
Securities Exchange Act (SEC),
 55
Seeger, Pete, **114**

segregation, **80, 85–86, 94**
September 11, 2001,
 terrorist attacks, **142–143**
settlement houses, **21**
Schultz, Dutch, **49**
Sinclair, Upton, **39**
Sioux Nation, **13, 14**
Sitting Bull, **14, 15**
Social Security Act (SSA), **55**
Somalia, **71**
Songs, **114**
South Korea, **82**
South Vietnam, **82**
Soviet Union. *See also* Russia
 after World War II, **77, 81**
 Cold War with, **82, 84,
  95–96**
 collapse of, **138, 141**
 Nixon's visit to, **118**
 space program in, **86, 97**
 in World War II, **67, 68,
  71, 74**
space exploration, **86, 97,
 99, 132**
space race, **86, 97, 99**
Spain, fascism in, **65**
Spanish-American War, **4,
 33**
Spanish Civil War, **65, 67**
Sputnik, **86, 97**
Stalin, Josef, **67, 83**
steel industry, **7**
stock market crash of 1929,
 52
Strategic Defense Initiative
 (SDI), **137**
suburbs, **125**
subways, **125**
Supreme Court rulings
 on English-language
  programs, **104–105**
 on presidential election
  of 2000, **139**
 on school desegregation,
  85, 94

Taliban, **142**
Tarbell, Ida, **39**

technological advances, **86,
 124–125, 132–133**
television, **86, 134, 135**
Tenth Amendment, **126**
terrorist attacks, **142–143**
textile industry, **6, 20**
Three Mile Island, **129**
Titanic, **133**
transportation, **6, 7, 11, 85,
 125, 132**
treaties, **13–14, 103**
Treaty of Versailles, **45, 67**
Triangle Shirtwaist factory,
 35
Truman, Harry S, **80, 81, 90**
Twain, Mark, **5**
Tweed, "Boss," **5**

United Nations
 creation of, **77, 81**
 environmental conferences
  sponsored by, **130**
 Iraq and, **138**
United States
 after Civil War, **4–5, 23**
 after World War II, **79**
 Cold War in, **82–84,
  95–97**
 how foreigners view,
  134–135
 international issues facing,
  141
 map of, **3**
 in 1920s, **49**
 in World War I, **42, 46**
 in World War II, **68,
  70–74, 76**
urban areas
 migration to, **37, 47**
 schools in, **39**
 shift to suburbs from, **125**
USA Patriot Act, **143**

V-E Day, **76**
Vanderbilt, William H., **5**
Vietnam, **71, 82, 104**
Vietnam War, **82, 111, 112,
 114**

Volunteers in Service for
 America (VISTA), **109**
voting rights, **47, 94, 109**
Voting Rights Act of 1965,
 109

"war on poverty," **109**
Warner, Charles, **5**
Watergate affair, **119**
Wells, Ida B., **47, 59**
West Germany, **77**
Wilson, Woodrow, **45, 60**
women
 employment of, **20, 34,
  94, 106**
 equal rights for, **106**
 voting rights for, **47**
 during World War II, **72,
  80, 94**
Works Progress
 Administration (WPA), **55**
World War I
 casualties in, **44**
 Europe during, **41, 42, 44,
  45, 64**
 events of, **43**
 treaty following, **45**
 United States during, **42**
 veterans of, **53**
World War II
 casualties in, **77**
 causes and effects in, **78**
 defeat of Axis powers in,
  76
 effects of, **77**
 Europe during, **67–69, 74**
 events of, **67–69, 71, 143**
 internment camps during,
  73, 94, 104
 United States during, **68,
  70–74, 76**

Zuni, **16**